The
Other Half
Further letters of Denis Thatcher

The Other Half

Further letters of Denis Thatcher

Written by Richard Ingrams & John Wells
Illustrated by George Adamson

PRIVATE EYE/ANDRE DEUTSCH

Published in Great Britain by Private Eye Productions Ltd.,
34 Greek Street, London W1.
In association with Andre Deutsch Ltd.,
105 Great Russell Street, London WC1.

Illustrations by George Adamson, © 1981

Designed by Peter Windett Associates.

ISBN 233 97420 2

Printed by Billing & Sons Ltd.,
Walnut Tree Close,
Guildford, Surrey.

10 Downing Street
Whitehall

9 MAY 1980

Dear Bill,

Forgive me for not answering all of your telephone calls during the crisis, but M. was hoping Carter would ring any minute on the hot line and things, at this end at least, were a trifle tense. I gather the Major was a bit carried away after the CD practice at Maidstone and was trying to get through for a nuclear sitrep. What the poor old bean doesn't quite grasp is that I'm often just as much in the dark as you lot. As indeed is M. She was absolutely hopping mad hearing about Carter's hostage rescue attempt on the wireless, but I pointed out that even Vance wasn't au fait with events so it was hardly surprising if Carter failed to give the tip-off to his friends and allies around the globe.

I don't know whether I've ever mentioned it before, Bill, but Carter has always struck me as a very rum sort of cove, ever since that time he went around holding hands with his wife. M. continues to go into bat for him in the H of C, but from where I'm sitting it's pretty clear he's a bit top-heavy on the loony end of things. Carrington admitted as much himself when he called in to collect his shoes which he left behind the week before. But his reading is that if Carter starts feeling unwanted and unloved something might crack and he'd press the red one. Hence the general closing of ranks and rallying round, even by Giscard who hates his guts. I suppose this is a sound approach. Do you remember the time Sticky's brother who was head of that big ball-bearings firm in the Midlands got it into his head that everybody had it in for him? Took all his clothes off and went through the ornamental flowerbeds outside the works with a Rotivator. They had to take him away. (Is he out? No matter.)

Boris is rather coming round to this Ayatollah bloke. As, I may say, am I. If you're going to have a sky pilot in the driving seat, far better the mad Mullah than some awful wet blanket like that prize ass Runcie. My own view of the Islam problem is that they made a great mistake from the word go by putting a ban on snorts. Four wives quite a sound idea if you've got the constitution that can stand it, but how they manage it

5

without booze, God only knows! I said to Carrington, if only these students and muftis and so forth were allowed the odd snifter, come half-past five the pickets outside the Embassy would melt away leaving the place wide open for taxi-borne rescue missions of a civilised nature. I don't know whether he passed on to Carter my scheme for parachuting in crates of the duty-free, but it seemed a good idea at the time. I mean, even you or I, Bill, would be whirling like bloody dervishes if we couldn't adjourn every so often for a sip of the sparkling sherbet, especially in the sort of weather they have down there.

What price M's Common Market initiative? I think Saatchi & Saatchi may have come up with the idea of the Big No, the general notion being that in times of economic disaster, inflation, mass unemployment etc there's a lot of mileage to be got out of being bloody to the foreigner. I suppose they know what they're doing. The Boss seems to me to be a bit prone to euphoria. I don't know about you, but I've always found this was rather a tricky time of year for all of us, and I'm sure you did the right thing by packing Daphne off to Martinique before the symptoms got too distressing. I blame that Jimmy Young chappie on the wireless. I went into the broadcasting place with M. and I didn't like the cut of his jib one little bit. All that bobbing about and smarmy talk inevitably goes to her head and then she comes out with some damn fool line about being another de Gaulle. Next stop Napoleon, what Bill? Still, I like to think I exercise a soothing influence.

A propos the Major's birthday celebrations on 14th May. I gather the plan is to RV for pre-lunch lotions at the Cat and Hamster in the Pantiles at 11.30 sharp. Technically speaking I am under house arrest that day, but Eric and Boris between them have devised an ingenious little escape wheeze which involves me donning a false beard and walking confidently out of the front door to be driven off by Boris in Arab gear at the wheel of the Rolls. (Eric meanwhile to create a diversion by sitting in my den hammering at the typewriter.) Boris says that anyone nowadays done up in wog paraphernalia gets auto-matic VIP treatment, waved through checkpoints without question etc, so the scheme should be foolproof. Fingers crossed nonetheless.

Yours aye,

DENIS

10 Downing Street
Whitehall

23 MAY 1980

Dear Bill,

I don't want to speak out of turn, but my clear impression is that we've got the buggers on the run at long last. I don't think I've had a chance to put pen to paper since the SAS dust-up at Prince's Gate. Best thing since the Coronation. High time a few wogs bit the dust and thank God there was a British finger on the trigger. I just hope that ass Carter recog-nises that when it comes to mowing down the Dervish Britain can still teach the rest of the world a lesson or two. By the by, did you feel a mite let down by old Whitelaw after the curtain finally descended? I know he was being got at by all those sneering little reptiles from Fleet Street but, as I said to M., why couldn't he come straight out with the joyful tidings about the wog cull, i.e. that the little fellows had been lined up in the corner and rat-a-tat-tat, and that the only reason the last one got out in one piece was that they thought he was one of ours? Instead of which, we got the pussy-footing stuff about sub judice and the Ministry of Defence. What's old Oyster Eyes got to be ashamed of? I told Carrington that if I'd had any say in it they'd have lugged them out, all two and a half brace of them, and had our masked friends from the SAS round for a photo-call with their boots planted on the day's bag. What, Bill? I'm beginning to think Whitelaw deep down may be a bit of a wet. A decent enough old stick and a demon with the mashie, no doubt, but inclined to fluff his putts.

If it hadn't been for our little contretemps on the Major's birthday I'd have had a damn good laugh over that other lot of untouchables, the TUC. What about little Murray, then, swanning it in Madeira when the so-called Day of Action is looming up? I don't know whether you recognised it from the photographs, but that was the hotel where Sticky got such a nasty bout of the Pharoah's Revenge in '69. He said it was the sea-food, but I suspected an overdose of the local hooch as usual. I remember it set him back £40 a night — even in those days, when £40 was a lot of money. A pretty classy sort of joint, and I must say I'd be pretty shirty if I was still on the Burmah Board, getting away from it all for a three-week mid-Spring mini-break, only to find the Cloth Cap Brigade sitting out there as bold as brass puffing a Corona Corona by the pool and snipping their snortoes in the Members' Enclosure. For once the Press johnnies did an absolutely splendid job bearding the little fellow and buggering up his holiday good and proper. I shouldn't think he'll go back to Madeira in a hurry. Next year Southend more likely, I'd have thought, Bill. Bag of whelks and a knotted hankie on the promenade would be more his line of country.

As to the schemozzle on the Major's birthday, the whole thing was a complete balls-up from the word go. You may remember the plan was for Boris to spring me from Number Ten, driving up to the front door in Arab gear while I strode out under cover of a beard. What I overlooked was that May 14th happened also to be the TUC's Day For Playing Silly Buggers. I generally see eye to eye with Boris, but when he came in with the early morning snort and a packet of fags on

a tray to announce that he was regretfully withdrawing his services in solidarity with the aspirations of something or other, I absolutely blew my top. To no avail, of course. One thing I've learned about the Russians from Peter Carrington is that once they dig their heels in there's no moving them. However, I was determined not to let the Major down and was just donning the Arab kit, prior to shimmering out of the front door as planned, when Eric came in and started kicking up the most godawful fuss about security. In the end he insisted on accompanying me in the passenger seat, wearing the false beard. I got to the garage without too much trouble, but no sooner had I screeched to a halt outside Number Ten and thrown open the door for Eric to scramble aboard than the Third World War broke out. Violent explosions, smoke, hooded black figures running to and fro, tin-openers applied to the roof, a complete re-run of the Prince's Gate lark, ending with self and Eric face down in the gutter, hands strapped behind our backs, listening to some straight talk from a chap in a balaclava helmet. Boss inevitably shirty about the whole thing, and my Insurance Company proving very tricky about what's left of the Rolls.

After it was all over I must say the Corporal in charge of the Squad was most apologetic, and after a few shots in the pantry we got talking about this that and the other. He said morale was very high in the Unit, and if only the Boss would blow the whistle he reckoned they could give the entire IRA the Prince's Gate treatment over a weekend, and everything would be tickety-boo. I promised to put in a word once things had calmed down a bit upstairs. Alas, M. is still fuming over our little escapade during old Tito's funeral. How was I to know that she'd be coming back on an earlier plane before we had a chance to get Maurice Picarda's musical lady friend out of the Cabinet Room? Ah well, these things are sent to try us, I suppose.

What about Royal St George's for the Open? We could stay in that very decent little pub in the Sandwich kept by the widow Venables.

Yours in the Pink,

DENIS

Dear Bill,

Flaming June, eh? A propos, did you see us on the TV? I
don't know whether I've mentioned two little wop fellows
who loom fairly large in M's life, but they're called Saatchi and
Saatchi — I think one's called Luigi and the other one's called
Alberto, but it could be the other way round. Anyway, whenever there's not much going on, they ring up and come oiling
in with some new publicity stunt.

I was dosing the greenfly out the back with that frightfully
good aerosol defoliant that Picarda got the recipe for from
some boffin on the run from Porton Down, and most of the
indoor staff being down at the betting shop it fell to my lot to
open the front door. Lo and behold the Corsican Brothers.
Shiny suits, carnations, rings a-sparkle on every finger, teeth
a-gleam. How nice to see me, great pleasure, arm pumped up
and down, waft of parma violets. Do you remember that
couple of spivs who used to hang about the nineteenth at
Huntercombe just after the war flogging nylons? Very much
the same style of cove.

The name of the game, it transpires on this occasion, is an
outing to Madame Tussaud's in the Marylebone Road to be
fitted out for the waxworks show. Pale pink Rolls at our disposal, the Brothers falling over each other among the cushions
in the back, opening champagne, demonstrating stereophonic
sound system, electric windows, just like a couple of monkeys.
Eric crammed in a corner of the back seat, looking very dis-
approving. Rolls purrs to a silent halt, welcoming committee
sidle out from the shadows. Lord Someone-or-other presented
with great relish by Luigi, or it may have been Alberto, and we
are all swept in under the canopy.

I hadn't been since the days when Uncle Jonah used to
dump me there while he popped off to his little rendez-vous
during the afternoons, but it's a pretty tatty sort of place, Bill.
What struck me was that it was impossible to tell who any-
body was actually meant to be. I thought I spotted old Wilson,
admittedly looking a bit waxen and glassy, but when I read the
label underneath it turned out to be Bertrand Russell. Any-

way M. seemed pretty taken by the whole set-up, good old laugh at the Royals etc, booze flows very freely, tape measures and calipers out, glass eyeballs produced from tray and held up for matching purposes, small samples of hair, eyebrows etcetera snipped away. In the end I began to quite enjoy it.

By the by, one of the Bertie Wooftahs on duty took me aside and explained how they do it. There being a pretty constant turnover in celebrities, and naturally wishing to save on the spondulicks, apparently, Bill, they recycle the bodies. Just between the two of us, M. was going to be knocked together out of an old Barbara Castle, and they'd got a Jeremy Thorpe that would be "just the thing" for me. Honestly, Bill, it gave me quite a turn, thinking of changing trousers with that bounder.

12

Come the great day of the unveiling before the world's press. Usual turnout from the reptile house, all well and truly lubricated by Luigi and Alberto prior to kick-off. I was standing there inspecting the exhibits, thinking that a sharpener wouldn't come amiss and trying to work out who was meant to be who, when I noticed M. whispering in an off-hand manner to Lord Tussaud and waving a hand airily in my direction. Whereupon, Bill, blow me if two burly little fellows in brown overalls don't move across the stage towards me, lift me sharply off my feet and before I can protest I am upended and bundled off, I presume towards the melting pot. Luckily a few brisk obscenities were enough to convince them of their mistake, and they put me down with no great ceremony, but not before the reptiles had sniggered their fill.

It turned out, Bill, that the Proprietor in her infinite wisdom had given instructions that yours truly was once more Not Wanted On Voyage in a Cabinet situation. However, as the rest of them look like something out of the window of the gents outfitters in Sevenoaks, I can't say I felt unduly miffed at the exclusion.

From your vantage point, Bill, it may look, in a more general context, as if we're on the rocks with this 20% inflation, recession looming, etc. All I can say is that you wouldn't think so if you were here. Optimism is the keyword, and come July the word is that everything is going to look different. The Mad Monk shouts with laughter from morning till night, Howe never stops giggling, and Stevarse minns about like a peacock on heat. According to the Brothers, whose business it is to look on the bright side of things anyway, the TUC and the Labour Party are tearing themselves to bits, and all we have to do is to sit back and count our winnings. Boris, I must confess, is very sceptical, and in my own experience, he's the only one who knows.

Do thank your friend in the construction business for the crate of Pimm's. I'm keeping it for our proposed meeting at this location.

Yours aye,

DENIS

Dear Bill,

I wonder how Daphne would feel about me coming to stay at Old Moorings for a few days? I feel a brief recuperation out of the front line might be to everyone's advantage, especially if the two of us can get in a few rounds of golf and generally re-fuel the tanks. Anyway, have a think about it — always assuming that Daphne's state of health can stand the strain — and let me know.

M., I must confess, has been pretty fraught of late, ever since the big Eurosummit, and even little Peter Carrington, out of whose arse the sun is normally deemed to shine like a beacon on Jubilee Night, has been sent to the doghouse. Personally I haven't followed all the matches in the league table to date — not, as you know, Bill, having much time for the foreigner in whatever shape or form — but according to Boris the Boss's plan was basically sound: i.e. veto the French farm price rises, throw your weight around, and in the end Brother Froggie will come to heel on the Contributions.

Accordingly, Tweedledum and Tweedledee, i.e. Walker and Carrington, twinkle off to Brussels with firm instructions to stand firm and resist all brands of continental flattery, free bottles of pop, evenings out at the Folies Bergeres and so forth. Instead of which, as Boris discovered before any of the rest of us on his short-wave wireless, the Twins caved in at an early stage, agreed to some botched-up compromise deal and caught the first train back to London.

As sheer bad luck would have it, Bill, I happened to be mooching around the Boardroom when the two of them were called in the following morning. All a-beam, hair glinting brightly in the sun, clearly thinking they'd done rather well for themselves. One glance at the Proprietor's face should have convinced them of their error. I knew from experience that a Force Eighter was on its way, and seeing for a change that I was not to be its victim hovered in the wings, pouring myself a sharpener in anticipation of a damn good show of fireworks.

My God, Bill, they certainly got it fair and square amidships! Did they think that M. had been to Dublin and points west, gone fourteen rounds with Giscard and Schmidt, put up with being vilified in the Froggie Prints as Madame Non, just in order to have the rug pulled from under her by a couple of cretins with a joint mental age of six? Why did she have to do all the work, could she never trust anyone to do the simplest thing if she didn't personally supervise? (This harangue being familiar, I should add, to yours truly, and making me feel sympathy even with a thoroughly obnoxious little HMG like Walker.)

To begin with Peter Carrington looked a bit hot around the gills, polished his glasses, and I thought might be going to take his punishment lying down. But just as I was about to step in and suggest sharpeners all round, his aristocratic poise suddenly deserted him. "Listen to me, you boring old bag" (ipsissima verba, Bill, as the lawyers would say). "If you think that Walker and I are going to spend the best years of our lives sitting up all night in Strasbourg with earphones strapped to our bloody heads in a roomful of Belgians haggling about the price of beetroot, you've got another think coming. Remember Rhodesia! I don't know whether you happen to have heard, but I have been hailed as the greatest Foreign Secretary this country has had since Palmerston. You're not talking to third-rate lobby fodder like Stevarse or Heseltine! Thank God I managed to inject a bit of class into your miserable bunch of suburban wankers. Well, that's it. I resign!" With that, the immaculately dressed little fellow hurled his briefcase into the air, ultimately to be fielded by Eric, and strode from the room, leaving Walker somewhat uncertain what iron to play next. Under cover of opening the door for Lord C., I withdrew to the attic and pulled up the ladder.

According to Boris's latest information, some kind of peace has been patched up, but the Boss has still got a very nasty light in her eye and I have been keeping the lowest of possible profiles at breakfast behind the *Daily Telegraph*.

I don't know if I told you, Bill, but ever since we got in there's a very odd little East End barrow-boy figure who lurks from time to time on the fringes of things here. Apparently he owns the *Daily Star*. He's constantly on the phone to Cosgrove or the Saatchi Brothers to find out what the Party Line is on this, that and the other and he strikes me, Bill, as an arse-crawler of the first water. Besides which — I don't know if you ever see it at the barber's — the paper he puts out is absolute Corporals' Mess stuff.

Well, Bill, you can imagine the shock to the system, given the prevailing mood of tension and despair, to be told that the same Cockney whelk-peddlar, whose name incidentally is Matthews, is to be dignified with the ermine. To tell you the truth, Bill, I was so taken aback that before I knew what I was saying I told M. she might just as well have given a peerage to Maurice Picarda's accountant — I can't remember his name but you know the one I mean, pencil moustache, trilby hat, padded shoulders, spent some years at Her Majesty's expense at Wormwood Scrubs. Crikey, Bill, straight through the clubhouse window with that one. You will now understand the reason for plea for asylum as outlined in para 1.

Yours in purdah,

DENIS

10 Downing Street
Whitehall

4 JULY 1980

Dear Bill,

I must say I did enjoy our little shindig here at Number Ten during M's summiting business in Venice. While the cat's away the mice will play, what? I was exceedingly glad not to have to trail along on that particular outing. I made enquiries and apparently the whole place is built on a lot of islands, so there's no golf course. Also, with all that dirty water sloshing about and the Eyeties emptying their gerries out of the window I'm told the pong is something shocking at this time of the year, besides which, as you know, that prize ass Carter was there, holding hands with his wife and exhibiting his grisly little daughter to the photographers. (Alberto Saatchi, who is my source, or it may have been Luigi, tells me that our American friends' latest wheeze is to dig up some old film star to take over. I think his name is Charlton Heston but I wouldn't be too sure. Really, Bill, it does seem a bit absurd! M. has her faults, God knows, but we would all think it pretty

odd if they wheeled in Frankie Howerd as a substitute. Don't you think?)

I'm glad to say that by the time the Boss flew back, Boris had the place roughly shipshape. The various nasty stains the Major left by flicking butter pats at the ceiling in the Cabinet Room barely notice, and you'd never guess that the old boy in the oil painting in the hall had had that moustache painted on him by Squiffy. M. did raise the question of the lavatory cistern being pulled away from the wall — that *was* Maurice Picarda, wasn't it? — but I blamed the terrible thunderstorms and painted a lurid picture of damn near being struck by lightning while behaunched. I could tell she didn't believe it for a moment, but there was no come-back.

At the time I didn't entirely understand the cause of Picarda's somewhat lachrymose condition. However, we had a long heart-to-heart last night, and things haven't been going too well for the poor old sod. You know his garage business blew up some months ago? Well, after that he hung about in Gozo for a bit until the coast was clear, and on his return started a small business selling some kind of solar heating equipment to our friends in the Gulf. I couldn't quite follow his sales patter on the phone, but apparently you have to attach some sort of umbrella contraption made of cooking foil to the chimney, plug it into the Serviwarm and Bob's your uncle: heating bills slashed and so forth. According to Maurice it couldn't possibly have gone wrong: conserving mineral fuels, boosting the export drive, precisely the kind of thing the Monk is always droning on about. Blow me, Bill, two weeks ago the bank manager starts bouncing his cheques. Not surprising, I suppose, when you think he was paying fifteen per cent on a couple of million. Ugly talk about bankruptcy, Maurice not absolutely certain in his own mind as to whether he'd been discharged after the last lot, so can you wonder, in the circs, if the chap takes a lotion or two too many to dull the heartache?

I took it upon myself to raise the matter with Howe when he was mooching about in his brothel creepers outside the Boss's den, waiting for the green light to come on. Apparently, as you may have seen in the gutter press, they've got some big pow-wow this week at which they're meant to be deciding what the hell they're up to, and about time too in my opinion. Anyway, buttonhole Howe, what about Picarda? Small business, always been one for initiative and enterprise ever since he started selling spare parts to the Army during the war, solar heating damn fine wheeze, good and faithful Tory, what's gone wrong? I don't know if I've mentioned it before, Bill, but Howe seems a bit slow on the uptake to me, like a lot of these lawyer johnnies, and for a long time he didn't seem to haul in what I was talking about. Hummed and hahed, scratched his bum, I helped myself to a sharpener, and he eventually condescended, no green light being forthcoming, to give Counsel's Opinion. Number One: overall target to bring inflation within manageable limits by the mid-nineties. Number Two: in order to achieve this, you do something called cutting the money supply. This is the bit I have never understood and, strictly between ourselves, Bill, I don't think Howe does either. The idea all stems from some little Californian guru called Milton Shulman. In the process, Howe vouchsafed, a whole lot of people — by this I presume he meant Picarda — are going to get their fingers burned. No U-turns, no going back, into the Valley of Death, etc. I was about to take issue with this on the grounds of basic sanity when the green light flickered and he sponged away across the polished floor clutching his briefcase with a somewhat haunted mien.

A propos your summer golfing proposal at the Royal and Ancient. I am going to do my damnedest to make up the foursome you propose but the Boss is already muttering darkly about traipsing off on her annual pilgrimage to stay with that awful old bird with the red face who owns the Isle of Muck. I honestly don't think I can stand it again after last year, and if the worst comes to the worst I'll try the slipped disc and appalling agony ploy. However, Saatchi and Saatchi are racking their brains about how to cash in on the Queen Mum's eightieth birthday racket, so the R&A may have to go by the board in favour of standing about outside Balmoral sipping the Duke's somewhat parsimonious tinctures. What a ghastly prospect!

Yours in the doldrums,

DENIS

18 JULY 1980

Dear Bill,

I don't know whether I've ever expatiated in our correspondence on this Prior bird. Red face, on the plump side, runs a farm somewhere near Colchester apparently. I always get on very well with him. He's not a golfer, but he likes a snort and he usually has time to chew the fat with yours truly, which is more than you can say for the Mad Monk or some of the other creeps we have through here. There was a bit of a rumpus last week, as you may have seen in the *Telegraph*, when he made the very reasonable suggestion that some of the unemployed layabouts you see hanging about outside the betting shop in any High Street could usefully be set to work washing sheets and cleaning out the bogs in the hospitals.

Honestly, Bill, you'd think he'd proposed compulsory castration for the entire proletariat. (Incidentally quite a good wheeze, but not an automatic passport to electoral success!) All the Labour yobboes up in arms, Tony Benn whistling like a steam kettle and wild talk of Forced Labour Camps. The trouble with the Socialists is that they're totally out of touch. The Major was telling me only the other day about a club near Folkestone where the greens are absolutely cluttered up with unemployed skinheads and punks playing on weekdays when the Members want to use the course. Picking up fifty quid a week on the dole and the green fees still peanuts in clubs like that, there's not a thing to stop them. What is worse, the Major says you can't get near the bar for the buggers lining up to order lemonade. So full marks to old Prior for trying to thin them out.

What puzzles me though, Bill, is where M. stands on Farmer Jim. He came round the other night about half past seven I should think. I was fairly well tanked up, having spent a fruitful afternoon watching the English Classic at Sutton Coldfield on the box, and was practising a few putts in the hall with my little indoor contraption from Lillywhites — did I ever show it you? — Boris retrieving the odd wild shot. In breezed Prior, a bulky file under his arm, weirdly enough quite

chipper at the prospect of meeting the Boss. All the same, I proffered a sharpener and we fell to talking about how you can't get a decent Cox's Orange Pippin nowadays for love or money and all thanks to Johnny Frog flooding the market with Golden Disgustings. Prior had accepted the other half and the time was passing very agreeably, everything tickety-boo, when the Boss flies out of her study looking as if raw meat alone will satisfy her.

"Now then, Jim, we've got no time to waste. We were elected on Union Reform and the Party isn't going to wear this cosmetic stuff you're proposing on the secondary pickets. Goodness me, we're all tired of leather-jacketed bully boys standing about outside factories full of perfectly happy people who want to do a decent day's work for a decent day's pay" — I could see Prior's eyes glazing over at this point, which didn't go unnoticed — "and making their lives an absolute misery." "Quite so, Mrs Thatcher," was our rubicund chum's rejoinder, "but remember what happened to friend Heath."

I think I've told you before, Bill, that the red rag effect of any mention of Old Sailorboy Ted is pretty predictable. Prior realised what he had done, and we both pulled our sou'westers down over our ears, patiently waiting for the storm to abate. Much of what M. said was personally offensive and very familiar to anyone who knew the form, and I think Prior had probably heard it all in Cabinet anyway. He hummed and hahed a bit, sipped his poison, nodded several times and finally, when there came a brief lull, handed the glass to me, looked at his watch and said that was all right then and M. could leave it with him. The Boss watched him go with rattle-snake eyes, looking not unlike the Chief Dalek about to exterminate and destroy. She then retired to her study to ruminate in solitary and didn't speak to one for several days.

I hesitate, as you know Bill, to put my oar in when it could only lead to further acrimony, but do you remember the drama at Burmah over the bridge school in the paint shop? Pegleg Ferguson stepped out of line on that one and was promptly given his cards by the Chairman. Then they brought in old Posner, as you recall, which wasn't a very happy choice, but that's another story. The peculiar thing about this set-up is that Prior has stepped further out of line than Pegleg ever dreamed of doing. The Boss slates him even on the telly when he must, all things being equal, occasionally be watching, but they still keep him on. There's no talk at all of telling him to get on his bike. Pretty odd. It did just cross my mind that she might be a bit scared of him. She couldn't be, could she? Boris thinks it's all a cunning ploy to keep both sides happy but, as you know, these politicos are a closed book to me. One some-times wonders how they'd manage if they had shareholders breathing down their necks.

A propos the Isle of Muck. According to Boris's sources, which are usually impeccable, there's not much hope of a reprieve. Which buggers up the Royal and Ancient. Also the Queen Mother hurdle remains to be cleared. Our holiday plans, in other words, highly classified, at least as far as I'm concerned. I do wish someone would tell me occasionally what the hell was going on. Bloody awful weather, what? I suppose Daphne's charity couldn't fly us out to some trouble spot in the tropics for a bit of peace?

Try and keep me briefed.

Yours aye,

DENIS

10 Downing Street
Whitehall

Dear Bill,

Forgive me for not coming to the phone the other morning but I was somewhat glued to the unfolding panorama of the British Open at Muirfield. Do you remember the time we played there? I think it was with that funny little money-lender friend of Maurice Picarda's. (Someone told me the other day that he was now President of the World Bank, which I must say I find pretty hard to believe.) If memory serves he was taken short around the ninth or tenth and very much upset some lady golfers in the adjoining copse. Happy days, what? I kept remembering it every time the cameras showed that particular little nook on the TV.

Apparently there's been a bit of a hoo-hah over the latest unemployment figures and some of the Left Wing johnnies have been getting very excited down at the Talking Shop. Wild talk about the Thirties and how miserable it all was. As I said to Boris, the stuff you hear nowadays is baloney for the most part. You and I were around then, Bill, and I thought we had a pretty good time of it, all things considered. Plenty of golf and parties, booze at seven and six a bottle, no servant problem, the lower orders used to call you Sir, everything tickety-boo. And if Chamberlain hadn't been such a damn fool upsetting poor old Hitler, I dare say the party would still be in full swing. However, that's all champers under the bridge.

M. seems to be keeping her head through it all very gallantly, I must say. I wouldn't like to have to stand up in that frightful bad breath they have down there struggling to make myself heard above the brawling of those Labour yobboes. Do you ever listen to it on the wireless? It's just like feeding time at the gorilla house the way they carry on, our lot not much better than the others. What I said to Boris is it's all letting off steam, really. If you go and stand outside the building itself, everybody's going about their business in a perfectly ordinary manner, not much thought given to two million unemployed, only real problem all those ghastly sweaty tourists laden down with orange haversacks trying to pull a fast one on the decent hard-working members of the British Hoteliers Association.

The other point the Labour buggers don't seem able to haul in is that being on the dole nowadays is by no means the romantic lark it was before the war. The Major was telling me only the other day about some Irish navvy who lives in a big house in a village near his brother's place in Wiltshire, picks up a hundred and sixty quid a week at the Post Office at some special supplementary rate or other, collects vintage cars, and when he goes on holiday to Tenerife they send it down to him by airmail. Even allowing for the Major's love of a tall story, it makes you think.

I mentioned the above to M. over a dish of tay following the shindig in the House, adding the other, to me, crucial point that in fact, if you look around, there are bags of jobs going begging. It's just that people nowadays are too damn choosy to take them on. Sticky, I know for a fact, has been advertising for weeks outside his local newsagent for someone to come and mow his lawn and muck out his daughter's ponies once a week, offering 75p an hour — well above the ordinary rate — and the only person to come forward was the wrong colour for the job, in Mrs Sticky's eyes at least.

Well, if M's policies are going to shake down a few idle sods into useful service to the community like mowing Sticky's lawn, then more power to her arm is all I can say.

Meanwhile the Monk appears to have wiped the froth from round his lips and come up with something quite sensible for a change. I refer to putting a bomb under the GPO. High time somebody did something, even if it's pretty cock-eyed like most of the Monk's schemes. According to Boris, all it amounts to is that if you want to buy a Donald Duck telephone set at the Army and Navy Very Expensive Gift Department, HMG will no longer stand in your way. Quite honestly, Bill, I never knew they did. Young Mark had one in his repulsive flat for years where you have to lift up a girl's skirt to dial the number. I distinctly remember telling him whatever you do, don't let M. see that, but I'd no idea it was against the law.

The other thing is delivering letters. Maurice Picarda was on in a great state of excitement as soon as it was announced, and he's setting up what sounds a very lucrative wheeze involving two ex-Borstal boys in his care on souped-up Japanese motorbikes, and he reckons that for a fiver a shot he

can guarantee same-day delivery anywhere within half a mile of Shepherd's Bush, where he is at present hanging out pending his latest bankruptcy proceedings. He thinks it may cause a bit of upward movement in the GPO's regular rates, but that's their own fault for being so incompetent. Those GPO sods have had it coming to them for years. If I've had one crossed line in the last month I must have had a hundred.

By the by, what about our chaps winning all those gold medals in Moscow? I drank to that, I don't mind telling you, and a pretty stiffish one, too. M. pointedly refused to join in the jollity, and even stopped Peter Carrington sending a wire to our lucky gong-wallahs. I said surely the best way to show the Russian Bear what we think about Afghanistan is to swim, throw things, and hop skip and jump better than they can. The fact is of course that we can't, not being stuffed with steroids and pep-up pills, but at least we can have a try.

Yours in high spirits,

DENIS

Stop Press: Royal and Ancient definitely a washout. Today we got the official summons to Balmoral. Bib and tucker, bring guns, fishing rods etc with view playing silly buggers up the Glen. God help each and every one.

10 Downing Street
Whitehall

15 AUGUST 1980

Dear Bill,

What price the enclosed snap from Bonnie Balmoral? I always thought wearing a kilt was a pretty daft idea, but they do save time in the Gents.

A pretty grisly outing all in all, Bill, as I foresaw. We arrived at the station, M. not having addressed a word to me since we left King's Cross, despite efforts on my part to establish cordial relations: delightful landscape, number of tunnels, cathedrals visible en route, etc. All to no avail. In the end I retired to the buffet and lined up a few British Rail miniatures which I quaffed with a very nice cove called MacLehose who sells Fairisle jumpers to the Japs. A fund of good tales, and a real wrench when he got off at Dundee, or somewhere of that sort — I can never tell those towns apart.

Anyway. Whisked off in one of the Royal limos to Balmoral. God, Bill, what a dump! I don't know whether you remember that loony-bin near Esher where the Major's father spent his final years, but very much the same kind of atmosphere. Long corridors, antlers all over the place, arctic even in mid-summer, a lot of burly old lags standing about in the local fancy dress ready to bite your leg off if you step out of line, and a three mile trek to the bog.

The House Party consisted of various Royals, several antique specimens of the aristocracy and, to cap it all, my least favourite sky-pilot, Runcie (and wife). By lunchtime on the Saturday my spirits were on the floor, snorts not being available in any great abundance, and it being my clear impression that the D of E, Queen Mum and Princess M. must have some secret supply, or at least a few bottles cooling somewhere offstage. I found no other explanation for their air of relaxed geniality and their being able to listen without any violent anguish to Runcie's views on embroidery. After lunch I was about to slope off to find a quiet corner for a kip, when M. snarled very firmly in my ear that HM was due to attend the Auchtermuchty Highland Games that afternoon and would take it in very bad part if I didn't turn out and "enter into the spirit of things". It was at this point that we all had to put on kilts (see pic).

The limos were duly brought out of the museum, and conceive of my delight when I found myself crushed into the back of a 1925 Daimler between Mrs Runcie and an overweight coon, some kind of ambassador or other from one of those African countries who had come for the lift. On arrival at Auchtermuchty we were greeted by the citizenry waving their flags, and took our places on a rather rickety tumbril draped in patriotic colours. Having sat through the Tory Conference at Blackpool I thought I could take anything, but after four hours of watching hideous women leaping up and down in kilts to the eerie wail of the bagpipes, Highland cattle being prodded by various grog-blossomed derelicts in tam o'shanters, and the usual Scots Porridge Oats stuff with the local Charles Atlas types dropping telegraph poles, my only consolation was to imagine one such being dropped very heavily on Mrs Runcie by my good self.

At about half past six the entire population lined up to sing a thirty-verse part-song in honour of the Queen Mum's four-score years. My God, Bill, you've got to hand it to her. Four weeks of that routine and I'd be in the drying-out unit. Seven o'clock came and went, local dental work still on display, spine-chilling discords and a cold wind getting up. Seven-thirty, refreshments in marquee. Hopes dashed to discover refreshments in question consist of fancy cakes and tea, provided by ample-bosomed ladies of the WVS. D of E very decently sidles up. "You realise I have to do this every bloody year, Thatcher, so you can count yourself lucky."

Princess M. leaning against a tent pole looking rather flushed, but still keeping her end up. M. herself getting on like a house on fire with one of the Charles Atlas brigade in a vest.

Dinner back at the Waxworks a pretty bleak business. We sat down about eight, I should think. All the local gentry winkled out of their castles to make up the strength, self by another overwhelming stroke of good luck stuck between two blue-rinse specimens, dentures and jewellery all a-glitter, heirlooms strung about their scrawny necks and much talk about grouse-shooting, milk yields and Highland adultery. Booze as ever administered in doses barely visible to the naked eye in cut-glass goblets made in the shape of thistles. At long last the ladies withdraw and the D of E enquires in ringing tones, "Come along Thatcher, what about one of your Clubroom tales, what?" Much laughter and thumping on table from assembled morons, fairly keen on taking the piss, I got the impression.

Meanwhile in the drawing room, roughly the size of Euston Station and just about as comfortable, Mrs Runcie had been prevailed upon without too much effort to play something classical. Nobody took a blind bit of notice, and fortunately it was barely audible above the roar of conversation. I was within a whisker of getting away behind a curtain unobserved when one of the blue-rinses grabbed me by the wrist and said it was time for Scrabble (apparently HM's idea of after-dinner fun). I don't know if you've ever played it, Bill, but it's like making up a crossword without any clues. Fawning and congratulations every time HM managed a three-letter word, lot of mockery when yours truly came unstuck on the spelling, and luckily the whole torment brought to an end when a brace of corgis came galloping in and overturned the board. The evening concluded with a bottle of quite decent stuff being opened and passed around in thimblefuls, after which the Queen Mum pinned me against the wall and almost cheered me up for a moment with a frightfully good story about the late Duke of Gloucester having to play golf with Haile Selassie and the Queen of Tonga at the time of the Coronation and them getting lost.

I thought last year's session on the Isle of Muck couldn't have been worse. Alas, not so. Next year, D.V., Benidorm.

Yours in extremis,

DENIS

10 Downing Street
Whitehall

29 AUGUST 1980

Dear Bill,

Thanks a bunch for your p.c. from Guadaloupe. I say, what a remarkably fine pair! The lady in question, though somewhat duskier of countenance, put me very much in mind of the barmaid at the Goat & Compasses at Sandwich in the old days. Vera, I think her name was, but I expect she's gone to the broker's yard long since, poor old thing. Luckily M. was late coming down that morning, so I was able to slip it into my dressing-gown pocket without the usual acrimony.

I imagine word has reached you of our little Dieppe raid. As you know, the Major had been on at me for some time to join him and Picarda on a day off the leash, the plan being for a trip across the Channel on the ferry, a slap-up beano at one of those big French watering-holes — five courses and fifty-seven varieties of booze, followed by a bracing eighteen holes at the nearby links run by a very decent expatriate accountant chum of Picarda's. After which, tinctures were envisaged prior to a real God Almighty blowout at a four-star establishment where they cook everything in alcohol, ending up with a tour of the waterfront nightspots, casino etc, and back home on the dawn hovercraft. Not a bad itinerary, I think you'll agree, Bill, and my only slight qualm was that your absence in tropical zones would mean that you could only be with us in spirit. Many a slip, however, twixt cup and lip, best laid plans etc.

M. had taken three days off at some damnfool health hydro at Virginia Water — a total waste of money if you ask me but Fatty Soames said he shed three stones there in a week and Saatchis have been leaning on her to do something about her chins — so the coast was clear. I drove the Humber down to Folkestone, taking on board the Major and little Picarda at the Flag & Anchor, and after a bracing snort or twain contre le mal de mer we drove the old bus onto the Sealink Ferry. Usual rather tripperish crowd on board, but we managed to commandeer a quiet corner of the bar on B Deck, and we were soon putting the world to rights with the help of an impressive army of miniatures.

At some point — I can't remember when, but we were certainly well out to sea — we found ourselves joined by a rather crusty old bugger from Roehampton who claimed he had been at school with me, though I couldn't for the life of me put a name to him. I find it pretty hard to put a name to anyone, quite honestly Bill, nowadays. Do you find that, as you get older? Eric, the priggish little twerp, says it's the drink but according to our GP, whose name funnily enough I can't remember either, about three billion brain cells burn off every year in any normal person after the age of nineteen. Anyway, this cove Mackevoy, or it may have been Patterson, had some kind of log stove business near Wokingham that was making a fortune, and he and Picarda immediately got on like a house on fire.

Time flew by and before we knew it the ship lurched violently to one side as all the ghastly trippers rushed to the rail to catch their first glimpse of La Belle France. We old codgers had seen it all before and decided to stay below. I thought something was up from the tone of the voices upstairs. The ship seemed to be stationary for rather a long time, and various incomprehensible announcements were made over the tannoy. Eventually the Major suggested we pop up on deck for a shufty.

I had always been under the impression, Bill, that one of the few things to be said in favour of our Gallic neighbours across the water was that they kept the lower orders in their place. From time to time the workers get a bit restless during the hot weather and start winkling out the cobblestones with a view to using them as offensive weapons, whereupon the Riot Police know exactly what to do and do it pretty damn quick. None of that Blair Peach nonsense over there. Well, all I can say is that that appears to be a thing of the past.

From where we stood on the deck you could quite clearly see the quayside awash with tiny black figures in berets and three days' growth of beard, behaving like bloody hooligans and not a gendarme in sight. As I said to old whatever his name was, the log-burner wallah, Grunwick all over again. Banners waving about, chanting of idiotic slogans in their incomprehensible lingo, and meanwhile progress of SS *Sibelius* effectively blocked by a barrage of little bateaux roped together, and weighed down to the gunwhales with more gesticulating Frogs, all yelling the odds about the price of Golden Delicious, or something else dear to their hearts.

The Major, to do him credit, took in the situation at a glance. No time to be wasted. Up the little steps to the bridge and a sharp word with Captain Olafsson, a shifty cove with a beard who looked to be the worse for drink, telling him to do his duty as a Norwegian and go full steam ahead through the fishing boats and get us to the restaurant before our table was given away to the natives. All to no avail, Bill. Grin grin from little Olafsson, "of course, gentlemen", next thing we know four burly matelots appear from nowhere and usher us below with no great ceremony. Another half hour elapses, a bit of parley-voo through the megaphone, one or two of the more spirited trippers lob the odd beer bottle at the Frog, fire is returned with airgun pellets and the Captain does a smart about-turn back to Folkestone. The Major, who by now is in a very nasty mood — the bar unaccountably having run dry — insists once ashore on buttonholing a bloke in the ticket office and asks for our money back. Thingummybob, the log-burner, does his best to restrain him before the police arrive, and we spend a very miserable evening in a horrible little pub down by the docks with a very loud jukebox, being sneered at by a gang of punks on their way to set fire to the pier.

I tell you, Bill, that's the last time I have any truck with Abroad. Sticky said it was just as bad going by air. He and Polly had to spend four hours sitting on the runway at Benidorm in a temperature of 106 degrees, screaming babies being sick all over them, and all because a couple of Spanish oiks with table tennis bats wanted a longer teabreak. I told M. when she got back from her hydro, looking pretty tetchy I must say, that this old country of ours may be a bugger's muddle but at least you can speak the language. Do tell, Bill, how did you manage in Martinique?

Yours agog,

DENIS

12 SEPTEMBER 1980

Dear Bill,

The more I see from this end of things the less I understand. I don't know whether the Major has been on to you about his chum Sharples who runs a biro factory near Chislehurst — you met him I think at that champagne beano given by the Oddfellows in Pershore — I dimly remember a cove with a ginger moustache drifting about rather the worse for wear, indeed I think he may have been our host. Any rate, the news is that the bloody bank has foreclosed and it looks like Carey Street. The point the Major made, and very emotionally, over the phone late the other night was that it was all our fault. If the kind of people who put M. in are going to the wall, what's it all about? To be quite frank, I absolutely agree.

I did in fact raise the matter with the Boss on the way back in the helicopter from our godawful trip to the Outer Darkness. The official reply, as far as I could gather above the roar of the rotors as we passed over Wick, was that if people priced themselves out of a job they'd only got themselves to blame. When I risked going on to point out that Sharples made his pile out of a handful of darkies, none of whom ever got more than thirty quid a week if they were lucky, I was told that there were bound to be some innocent casualties in the war against inflation.

It always comes back to this notion of the money supply which, for the life of me, I find extraordinarily difficult to grasp. Ever since we got in, according to little Howe and our old friend Rasputin, the plan has been to cut the money supply. But there it was in the pilot's copy of the *Daily Telegraph*, Money Supply on the Up and Up. No exchange controls, spondulicks flooding in from bloody everywhere. What worries me, Bill, is that I don't honestly think that our lot understands it either. Like Poland. I mean, they're all cock-a-hoop in this neck of the woods about the wonderful little unions and bully for them getting the right to strike. All exactly the kind of thing we're supposed to be one hundred per cent opposed to. I thought of raising this, too, but the firm line of M's mouth and the fact that she was busy making notes for a speech on the back of her sick bag made me think we'd probably had enough of politics for one day.

I don't know whether you've heard of a cove called Goldsmith, Bill — I think he was one of those rum customers who used to hang about Wilson, like that mackintosh chappie who is currently out on bail. They all got knighthoods and things out of that secretary woman of his. (I always felt sorry for the wife.) Anyway, blow me down if this Goldsmith, who runs a lot of off-licences and cash-and-carry places up and down the country, hasn't thrown a great beano at the Savoy for some rag, as I gather, that they give away free in the supermarkets, and has the brazen effrontery to try and dignify the occasion by inviting M. to make major speech on state of the nation! To put the tin hat on it, M. has said yes. I lay the whole thing at the door of our friends Saatchi and Saatchi, who'll do anything for the odd bob but, emboldened by a sharpener, I did say en passant to M. that she shouldn't touch this bloke with a bargepole. Scatty Longhurst, Sticky's broking friend, says there's been some malarkey about share dealing and, although I've learned from painful experience never to believe a word Scatty says, a lot of very decent blokes apparently did get their fingers badly burned a year or two ago. Anyway, bib and tucker and limo at the door for Wednesday night, whole thing promises to be a pretty good shambles and more anon.

What else shall I tell you? Oh yes. I always said I had a pretty good nose for a rotter, Bill. You remember a week or so ago I mentioned the little East End johnny who owns the *Daily Express* that M. for some inexplicable reason gave a peerage to? I said to Boris at the time he was a wrong 'un. Would you believe it? I was absolutely right. Last week tremendous rumpus, turns out this Whelks fellow, under cover of darkness, has paid a gang of hooligans to knock down that lovely old Firestone factory on the Great Western Road. We always used to pass it before the war on the way out to Sonning in Eddie Gorringe's drophead coupe. Those were the days, eh? Do you remember the night Sticky got locked in the khazi at the French Horn and we had to take the door off with your Number Five Iron? I think after that we were somewhat non grata with Mine Host. Sowerberry? Hampton? I can't remember his name, but I know he bought it during the Blitz, poor old bean.

I am going to do my damnedest to go AWOL on the Great Pow-Wow at Blackpool this year, so you might pencil in a tentative date for our little jaunt to Folkestone. Maurice Picarda has just managed to raise the wind to open a hotel and conference centre down there and I feel we ought to lend support.

Yours aye,

DENIS

10 Downing Street

Whitehall

26 SEPTEMBER 1980

Dear Bill,

I think I closed last time on a note of despondency at the prospect of a beano at the Savoy given by some jumped-up supermarket wallah called Goldstone. I mentioned, as I recall, that I had a few misgivings re the aforesaid. Scatty Longhurst, you may remember, was peddling some pretty fruity stories in the club, and when we got to the Savoy I must say my worst suspicions were confirmed. You've never seen such a bunch of sharks, Bill. It reminded me very forcibly of the turnout at old Barrington's funeral in Maidstone on the occasion the Wake was raided by the police. Apart from the obvious flotsam like Slater and that ghastly woman with the teeth who's always on the television, the rummest cove of all was a Safari Park johnny from Hythe called Aspinall, who turned out to be a great buddy of the titled chap in Belgravia who took an axe to his au-pair. Not to mention that frightful nancy-boy bishop with the blue-rinse hair — Stockwell or some name like that. Saatchi and Saatchi shimmering about like a couple of monkeys on a stick exulting at the rich haul, so I took the liberty of telling them that the television cameras should under no circumstances be allowed to dwell on the assembled throng if Margaret was ever to hold her head up in public again.

Entre nous, I formed the impression that the Goldstone man was absolutely barking.

Meanwhile the ebb and flow through the corridors here at Downing Street has been fairly frantic. Venturing down from the attic to replenish supplies I came across the new CBI bloke, Pillock I think his name is — used to be in Used Cars in the Midlands somewhere — combing his hair in the downstairs gents. Quite a decent sort from all appearances. He spotted me as a potential friend at court, and did a pretty thorough lather job on how everyone that matters is having his balls squeezed by this 16 per cent MLR business. I rather took the wind out of his sails, I think, by saying that I was doing quite nicely with my deposit account at the NatWest and quoting old Furniss's dictum about not running up bills at the bank. Anyway, he sloped in for a chinwag with the Boss, I could hear the sound of feathers flying, and although he came out with a flea in his ear I formed the distinct impression they will knock it down a bit to keep things sweet where the big loot comes from.

I think I've told you this before, Bill, it all comes back to this money supply mumbo jumbo and something I find absolutely baffling called M1, M2 and M3. I got stuck between Whitelaw and poor old Hailsham the other night, and asked them if they could shed any light. Hailsham gave a funny sort of laugh and went back to sleep, and old Oyster Eyes, I swear to you, Bill, pretended he hadn't heard and launched off on a pretty tedious harangue about what he wants to do to soccer hooligans.

By the by, old Peter Carrington would appear to have blotted his copybook at long last. It appears, though I only have Boris's version to go on, that there have been a lot of rumours floating about to do with a bit of dirty work down on the Gulf involving some randy South African sawbones and a body that needed a bit of explaining. Instead of keeping quiet and waiting for the whole thing to blow over which these things in my opinion are prone to do — the reptiles of Fleet Street being a fickle crew who never stay long nibbling at the same carcase — up pops Little Lord Fauntleroy in his best pinstripes and issues a twenty-nine point denial, whereupon all hell breaks loose and the ratpack come out of their holes again, blinking in the daylight, and fasten their infected teeth in his leg. I can't quite see why he felt obliged to speak up for the sawbones. As I've said before, the trouble with our Old Etonian friends is that they have no idea of how life is actually lived. You or I, Bill, would have a pretty good inkling in a flash of the type of person you'd find buzzing round the Arab honey-pot. Like that ex-RAF type, Wilmot I think his name was, who went out to Abu Dhabi for the Major with those chemical toilets before it all blew up in his face. A wrong 'un if ever I saw one. I could tell at once from his moustache. Not so the Superstatesman, Lord C. Pity, Bill, because otherwise I've always liked the cut of his jib, and we've had a good few snorterinos on the quiet in the back pantry and always got on like a house on fire.

Brighton looming up, and to date no very concrete prospect of escape. Didn't Sticky use to belong to a club somewhere up near the Devil's Dyke, or is my memory playing tricks with me yet again? If so, any chance of you joining me for a few quiet holes while the Boss is on her hind legs?

Nil desperandum.

Yours aye,

DENIS

GRAND METROPOLITAN HOTEL
BRIGHTON

10 OCTOBER 1980

Dear Bill,

What a hell-hole this is, Bill! I remember it before the war, when it was full of fossilised old Indian Army specimens with their memsahibs dribbling out the twilight of Empire on the prom. Now it's been taken over by some jumped-up little Eyetie who's painted it all in assorted garish hues. Muzak in the bogs, carpet on the walls and leather-style banquettes. M. is absolutely in her element. If I had the choice, we'd be in the Pig & Whistle up by the station which is still run by a native — I think he said he was in the RAF with Percy Topplemore. He certainly had one of those handlebar moustache numbers — and at least the place hasn't been refurbished.

I did have a last ditch moment with the Boss as to whether I could be excused parade, especially as all I have to do is sit on the platform grinning like a Barbary Ape and throwing myself about clapping like a madman whenever anyone opens his mouth. Application refused. It turns out that those frightful little creeps the Saatchis have done a special report for the Boss proving that yours truly is now a major electoral asset, achieving the same score as Captain, the Wilsons' cat. Boris told me that Alberto and Luigi have even got together various unemployables to stop people in the street, show them a photograph of me and ask them who it is. All I can say, Bill, is

I hope our scaly friends from Fleet Street don't get hold of that one, or I shan't be able to show my face at St George's ever again. Imagine the gales of laughter from the Battle of Britain boys.

As you would expect, M's lot were all very cock-a-hoop about the shambles at Blackpool last week. A propos, did you see Benn in action on the box at all? He put me in mind of that new friend of Margaret's with the German name who runs the supermarkets. Very much the look of poor old Tuppy Hetherington before his missus had to enlist the help of the men in white coats. I'll never forget the afternoon he shed his tweeds on the fairway, snapped all the Major's best clubs over his knee, and ran gibbering off into Guildford without a stitch on. Old Benn has much the same air about him. I can't believe he's a plausible alternative to Jim, but M. has very high hopes. The man they're scared of is the one with funny eyebrows that chap on the telly is always impersonating. The Major says he takes photographs of himself sitting in bedrooms, so I think there may be something pretty rum somewhere. The only one of their lot I ever liked was George Brown, and now he's on the wagon he's unbearable. Exactly what happened to Bomber MacLehose, if you remember. Went TT and is now the biggest bore in East Sussex.

The one M. starts foaming at the mouth at whenever she pops up on the gogglebox is the Shirley woman, who looks to me rather a good sort. But I can see M's point: one Wonder-woman is enough to be getting on with. M. keeps saying she's going to have to go to the hairdresser's before she can be taken seriously as a political rival.

Anyway, the logical upshot of all this, according to Boris, is that M's wets are in for a trouncing. Time to come out in our true colours, etc. Talking of which, you should see some of the people hanging about down here in Brighton. A lot of the younger MPs are pretty good yobboes, as I suppose is inevitable nowadays, all accompanied by brassy tarts; the usual so-called Party Workers, i.e. garage proprietors, night club owners and the Maurice Picarda brigade, not to mention the Fleet Street reptiles having a field day, all reeling about blind drunk, sniggering in anticipation at the thought of one making some sort of gaffe. I have therefore spent a good deal of the time here in the Walt Disney Suite — which is, thank God, equipped with the one colour television set in the whole of Brighton that gets something other than the Conference —

tuned in to Wentworth, and taking advantage of the very liberal trickle of snorterinoes brought in by a succession of Maltese waiters.

My stints on the platform, as you can imagine, are sheer unmitigated hell, and my jaw aches with smiling. Particularly when that ginger one, Heseltine, is up there spouting his frightful gibberish. He always goes down best, which wiil give you some indication of the type of person that constitutes the rabble.

I see there's something coming up in Estoril in November. I just might be able to shimmer out for a day or two without it being noticed, so it might be worth alerting Mrs Chancellor at the travel agency to see if she's got anything in the way of package cheapies.

Did you see the FO sent us out to Athens? All very badly blitzed still, and not a bunker in sight. Neither M. nor I had a blind idea why we were there.

Yours till the cows come home,

DENIS

10 Downing Street
Whitehall

24 OCTOBER 1980

Dear Bill,

How extraordinary we should have run into each other at the Birmingham Motor Show! Did you decide to buy the Fiesta in the end? I could see Daphne was getting on like a house on fire with the salesman. They are jolly good little cars, if economy is the name of the game. Maurice P. swears by them. He used to drive on in his ballpoint days before the chemical toilet fiasco in the Gulf.

In view of our VIP status I couldn't really linger. Saatchis had given the Boss seven minutes and she was due to do her lap of honour in the new Metro just as you were embarking on your very interesting tale of life out East. Edwardes, the rather smarmy little South African johnny who runs Leylands, told me that they're cock-a-hoop about advance orders and

claims 83mpg, which I find hard to believe. Also bags of room for a crate or two of the snorterinoes, but, needless to say, those bloody shop-stewards haven't wasted a moment before torpedoing the whole bang shoot by embarking on a nation-wide work to rule just because some idle bugger chooses to take a three hour teabreak. I keep telling the Boss one of these days they're going to have to pull the plug on that lot, Metro or no, and concede victory to the Nips. Poor old McIllvanney who bought it with Wingate's mob will be turning in his grave, but at least it'll teach those Moscow-subsidised vermin in the TUC a lesson or two.

Talking of the Congress, you probably saw that we had the smelly socks brigade round for tea and cakes a few days back. I told the Boss it would achieve precisely sod all, but Saatchis were keen on a bit of window dressing. What a shower, Bill! You or I wouldn't employ one of them as nightwatchman, let alone a caddy. Little Len Murray seems a decent enough chap, but between ourselves I don't think even he has the slightest idea of what's going on. The one who really gets up my nose is the Welsh cove with the whiny voice and glasses. Thinks he knows all the answers. Breezed into Number Ten, bold as brass, grinning like a Cheshire cat, and before I knew where I was the bugger had his arm round my shoulders and was blowing in my ear, enquiring whether we had anything stronger on the premises than a tea-bag. I don't know about you, Bill, but I've always had my doubts about the Taffs, and Jenkins is a typical specimen of the breed. Anyway, the Boss took them all into the Cabinet Room, flanked by the Monk, Brother Howe and Farmer Prior, leaving yours truly to entertain the bloody chauffeurs in the pantry. Shocking tales they told. They don't mind hanging about outside the Ritz until half past three in the morning if it's a gent, but they're buggered if they're going to do it for the tribunes of the plebs.

The thing I can't understand, Bill, is that when we moved in M. made it pretty clear to those Union hobbledehoys that the days of wine and roses at Number Ten were over, but here we are going through the motions just like Wilson and Callaghan. Alberto Saatchi, the one with the moustache who smells of Parma violets and is always picking his teeth, promised me it wouldn't happen again. Apparently all that transpired when they got in there was that the Boss laid it on the line about two and a half million unemployed being all their fault. The Monk frothed at the mouth in sympathy, Howe sat there beaming like an owl, and no one else got a word in edgeways. As he was going out little Len Murray whispered in my ear that I had his deepest sympathy. Cheeky little monkey.

A propos the roughhouse on the other side, the general whisper at this end is that Healey has got it in the bag despite efforts to discredit him with his followers by effusive support from our lot. There's some doubt about the way the withered old party with the long white hair and the bottleglass specs will turn. Foot. Perfectly decent chap. I've bumped into him a couple of times at cocktail parties. Spends his time in second-hand bookshops and walking around Hampstead Heath, but otherwise as normal as you or me. All the pinkoes think he's the bee's knees for some reason. But as I may have observed before, Bill, there's nowt so queer as folk in politics.

Do thank the Major for the duty-free; I'll try and have a word with Heseltine about his demolition difficulty but Boris tells me that Gothic Churches normally carry some sort of damnfool protection order.

Happy motoring.

Yours aye,

DENIS

10 Downing Street
Whitehall

7 NOVEMBER 1980

Dear Bill,

I expect you and Daphne have been having a good chuckle re the Royal Tour of Morocco. Hats off to H.M. and the D. of E. for kicking up a shindig over the frightful wog with the sunglasses buggering them about from arsehole to breakfast table. As one who has had his fair share of being kept waiting by that type of person, and being expected to grin and bear it, I gave them full marks for sounding off in the way they did. It surprised me because I'd always thought Hussein was a gallant little bloke who went to Harrow and was rather one of us. Clearly the hot climate and all that fornicating has taken its toll.

Back at the talking shop, storm cones have been hoisted in no uncertain manner. I hope you don't think I harp on about this too much, Bill, but it all goes back to this Money Supply mumbo-jumbo introduced by the little American fellow, Milton Schulman. It's pretty good eyewash, but the point is that they've all worked themselves up into a tremendous state about the fact that it isn't working, whatever it is. Anyway, the boffins in Whitehall have told them that they've got to find another two thousand million in the way of fat to be chopped off if their scenario is to have a hope in hell of turning out as predicted. The snag being, of course, that M. has always stuck to her guns on the Iron Lady stuff, standing up to the Russian Bear etc., and whatever happens no cutbacks at the Warbox.

Imagine our consternation then, when Eric, who takes the *Guardian*, pipes up at breakfast-time with the news that the Brasshats are all in a lather.

44

Cuts are in prospect and someone has leaked. Traditional Force Eighter, M. on the line within minutes to McNee, putting a hefty-ish price on the head of the mole. High dudgeon, inevitably, when it turns out that the prime suspect is the Chief of the Imperial General Staff, and not some little half-arsed Trot working in the cipher room as we had been led to believe. Red faces all round, M. decides to get her revenge by sending in the Army to muck out the latrines at Parkhurst. Rather childish, entre nous, but very much par for the course.

Meanwhile poor old M. has been getting a lot of flak from various parties anxious to loosen the corset and bring down the interest rates. As you know, Bill, my thinking on this matter is a trifle confused, torn as I am between the prospect of Maurice Picarda and his like going under again and my own steadily accumulating deposit account at the NatWest, still flourishing very impressively on 14%. However, I am a bit suspicious, quite frankly Bill, about some of the coves urging a respite for the boxwallahs. There's a fat cat called Rippon who used to be in very big with Heath and who now floats round the City dispensing unsolicited advice at sundry board meetings; there's Heath himself, who, as you know Bill, I have always considered an absolute bounder and four-letter fellow of the first water who refused to join the team and now hangs over the green sniggering every time someone muffs a putt. And that old walrus Macmillan. His piping up from beyond the grave, telling the Boss to turn again before we all end up in the soup, did strike me as pretty rich, particularly as M. had been so decent about wheeling him out as Exhibit A on every con-ceivable occasion. Whatever happens, entirely off the record, it's now pretty certain in my reading of the situation that we're in for another hike on the booze and fags front, so tell Daphne to take the hatchback down to the cash-and-carry and stock up with Yule in mind. To think all that's looming up again, Bill!

On a brighter front, we all had a jolly good laugh about *The Times* being put up for sale. Serve the little buggers right, I say: living like fighting cocks at the expense of some decent Canadian businessman who made his money the hard way. I keep telling M., the sooner she does the same with British Leyland the merrier for us all. Wouldn't you like to see the smiles wiped off the faces of those dreadful louts at Long-bridge? I can't see why the CBI gets so windy about unemployment. Never done you or me any harm, Bill, and I'm sure a lot of them could be shunted into Double Glazing. Picarda says there's a lot of call for it from people wanting to cut down on their fuel bills. He's rather keen on me joining the board of a new company he's floating, Picwarmth. Do you think I should?

Chin chin, old lad.

Yours,

DENIS

10 Downing Street
Whitehall

21 NOVEMBER 1980

Dear Bill,

A few shocks and surprises since I last put p to p, though on the American Election front I could have told them all along that Reagan would leave Carter hacking about in the rough by the first hole. I may have mentioned this before, but I've always said there was something very rum about a chap of Carter's age going about holding hands with his wife in public, and obviously the Yanks as a whole thought the same.

All in all, the OAPs appear to have cleaned up. As you can imagine, the beleaguered garrison at this end are chuffed to naafi breaks about old Foot being wheeled in by the Reds. The fear always was that the big burly chap with the eyebrows would make mincemeat out of the Boss, be viewed as credible alternative by the electorate as Mad Monk piped us further and further up the garden path, etc. Somehow they don't see this happening with the windswept old philospher at the helm, especially now he's got one foot in plaster. Jolly bad luck, actually. That sort of thing can happen to anyone at half past eleven at night, witness the fate of Tubby Arkwright the time he did his Cresta Run down three flights of stairs after the Oddfellows' do at Maidstone and had his neck in traction for the best part of a year.

Personally, as I think I said before, I can't make old Foot out at all. Over a glass of sherry a perfectly decent bird, sort of batty old party you quite often see just when you're about to drive off tottering across the Right of Way muttering to himself. But get him up on a soapbox and he does talk the most awful balls. I can only think it's intended to curry favour with all those long-haired Trots, because he comes from perfectly respectable West Country stock, brother in the Colonial Service who did splendid work riding round on a horse in Cyprus and cracking down on that mad sky-pilot with the funny hat and the beard. Boris for some reason thinks he's the best thing since sliced bread but I find myself utterly bewildered. He can't really think that he himself would have any sort of a life under the regime he proposes with the proles in charge.

As for the CBI shindig, I've been keeping my head down and stonewalling away whenever questioned. I used to see quite a lot of those chaps in Burmah days, and as drinking companions there's not a word to be said against them. Personally, though, I've always thought it was a mistake for us humble Boardroom buffers to get up on our hind legs in public, especially after three or four hours of knocking it back in the snug at these bally conferences. Incidentally, you notice how everyone, including our lot, picks on Brighton for their get-togethers — the thought uppermost in most of their minds, if you ask me, being a week away from the wife at the firm's expense and not having to drive home in the small hours after a number of Snortoes de Luxe.

You know my views on the interest rate, Bill, NatWest and so forth. As far as I can see, all the people who are squealing now are the ones who have been foolish enough to get into the red, spending money they haven't got, and it's a bit rich of cocky little Edwardes to start lecturing the Boss about how to set her house in order. By Christ, Bill, after all the blank cheques the Monk has handed over to keep those lazy goodfornothings at British bloody Leyland in colour tellies and cocktail cabinets crammed with booze, you'd think he'd have the decency to pipe down. As for that chap at Ford's, Beckett, I've never really thought much of their cars. You remember all the trouble you had with the Escort which broke down on the way to Plumpton that afternoon we had the cert?

However, that said, the Boss is plainly giving them as

good as she gets. There was a knees-up· here the other night in honour of the Queen Mum, bib and tucker, decorations will be worn, candelabra out of the bank, etc., extra catering staff from Stevarse's Rentaserf firm. Quite a jolly sort of beano as it turned out, with the old girl firing on all cylinders and coming out with a few very ripe stories — amazing at her age, when you come to think of it, Bill — and blow me, who comes in at the coffee and cigars stage but that oily little monkey Heseltine, asking everyone for twenty-one quid in used notes. The Queen Mum clearly thought it was a scream and gave him a handsome tip, but you can imagine the consternation among some of our more po-faced members. M. explained to me afterwards that it was something Saatchis had thought up for the press, the idea being that if we're going to give the firemen a fiver on the end of a string we have to show that we're able to take a joke ourselves. Or something like that.

Meanwhile M. blazes on, unswerving and undaunted. What the Becketts of this world fail to understand is that it's all that fat idiot Heath's fault. Once he's stuck his ugly nose in there's not a hope in hell of the old girl performing a U-turn or anything else. I haven't ventured into the connubial chamber of late, but I form the clear impression a little wax model of our seafaring friend may be receiving some fairly intensive acupuncture treatment in the long dark hours.

I don't suppose there's any chance of a brief excursion to parts unknown? I always believe it's a good idea to make oneself as scarce as possible during the somewhat tense run-up to Yule. Brochure enclosed.

My best to you and yours,

DENIS

5 DECEMBER 1980

Dear Bill,

Forgive me for going off the air for the past few days, but the balloon has rather gone up and we are all being shat upon from a considerable height. To tell you the truth, I'm not 100% certain as to what is actually going on, but I draw comfort from the fact that I am by no means alone in this! (Even Boris has moments when he is bewildered by it all.)

What I can't make out is the sudden decision to gang up on poor little Howe. As I may have told you, Bill, he's quite a decent bird, a lawyer with a rather talkative wife and depressingly abstemious habits, at least when M. is watching. For months and months everybody has been badgering the poor little bugger to do something about the interest rates, including yours truly on behalf of poor old Maurice, who has alas once again come to grief, this time in double-glazing, when the bottom fell out of Picwarmth.

Well, last Monday, friend Howe finally plucked up courage and snipped off two per cent. Crikey, Bill, you'd think after all the bullyboys banging on for so long about it this would have merited at least two feeble cheers from the red-nosed old buffers on the back benches. Not at all. Positive screams of rage and anguish, cries of debag Howe, out with the Cherry Blossom, etc. In my experience this often happens. Do you remember that song the barmaid in The Waggonload of Monkeys at Great Missenden was singing all that night we got inveigled into the darts match by those frightful Americans? "Once you've got what you want you don't want it after all", or something on those lines. As you know, Bill, I'm not one for philosophy, but there's a lot of truth in it. Although, if you ask me, many of those currently slinging the shit at poor old Howe are actually doing so out of pique at what's happening to their little nest-eggs at the NatWest. A propos, I was talking to a City type in the Club the other morning, and he was saying that there was no point in deposit accounts anyway, as the taxman takes it all, and the best thing to do is to channel the stuff into Jap stocks. I'm seeing Palfreyman, M's accountant, about this on Monday to ask him what he advises.

Be that as it may, Howe staggers back from the House, trousers askew, only to find the Proprietor in flesh-eating mood. Some Civil Service johnny, it turns out, has slipped in under the mat an edict to the effect that National Insurance contributions are in for a hike. Howe, pathetic little sod, reading from his prepared brief, of which, if you ask me, he doesn't understand a blind word, has given everyone the impression that only the proles are going to have to fork out on this occasion. The odd whimper from the Reds, but otherwise not a sound. Next thing, roars of apoplexy from the Wealth Creators. Some diligent soul, poring over Hansard in a moment of ennui, has discovered that the Employers, contrary to all Howe's assurances, are also going to have to reach fairly deep into the dungarees. Howe's pinstripes once again torn to the floor, the tin of boot polish out again, Carrington, Walker and all the usurers yelping for blood, why weren't they told? The Boss lending her shrill tones to the hue and cry.

Personally I feel a bit sorry for Howe. Half the time, you see Bill, these chaps are reading out bumf that has been thrust into their hands a split second before by the faceless men of Whitehall, and it's a miracle to me when they make it even sound like English. You remember the trouble you and I used to have presenting the Annual Accounts when we were on the board at Burmah: blurring rows of figures, meaningless platitudes, bloody accountants whispering in your ear at the last minute to move the decimal point three places to the left, refer to Appendix F to see true state of affairs, etc. Well, just imagine having to do that with the kind of money these people have at their disposal, particularly in that malodorous monkey house down by the river. No wonder they come to grief once in a while. There they are, spouting away, and in almost every case it's ventriloquist's dummy time. Same with H.M. The Queen. Same, I regret to say, even with M. Not content with Saatchi and Saatchi telling her what to say, she has now taken onto the permanent strength some superannuated theatrical hack in a dressing gown and a long cigarette holder to spice up her speeches with so-called jokes. I told her, in a moment of bravado while she was putting her hair in curlers the other night, that if she wanted that sort of thing why didn't she ask you and me to put our heads together over a few snorts, as we did for that very successful smoker at the Rotary do when the Major dressed up as a woman and sang that song about the rhubarb. I bet you we'd come up with something better than "The lady's not for burning", which nobody got anyway, though they all dutifully fell about clapping like sea-lions at the Zoo.

Xmas plans still wrapped in mist, but it looks horribly like Chequers again, and I know for a fact that they haven't fixed the central heating.

Abyssinia,

DENIS

10 Downing Street
Whitehall

19 DECEMBER 1980

Dear Bill,

I'm beginning to think that Christmas, bloody as it indubitably will be, may not come as such a bad thing after all. At least I should be able to manage a quiet day propping up the bar at the Waggonload of Monkeys in Great Missenden, and anything would be preferable to life at the Talking Shop at the moment, which is quite frankly hell on wheels.

You probably read about M's Mystery Tour to the Emerald Isles, about which there's been a good deal of idiotic speculation by the alcoholic wrecks in the Press Lobby. Having been on the trip, I am in a position for once to impart a few nuggets of fact, unlikely though these may seem at your end.

You know my views about our friends the Bogtrotters, Bill. Ever since we came in I've been urging the Boss to hack through the mooring ropes, cast the little buggers loose, green and orange, leave them to fend for themselves, tear each other limb from limb etc etc as is their traditional wont. As it is, a whole lot of our Income Tax is being syphoned off to maintain a military presence at the sharp end, having bricks thrown at them by a lot of curly-headed yobboes, paid for from cradle to grave by you and me, when they should be grappling with the Russian Bear.

I remember, when I was asked down to Deal by old General Wenham, his boy was back on leave and he said he'd rather be struggling through the mosquito-infested swamps of Borneo being picked off with poison darts than have to be cooped up in the Bogside, listening to that stupid prat Paisley blethering on ad nauseam. According to him, both sides are the most frightful clowns. The Prods, as they call them, aren't CofE at all, but some sort of Baptists who dress up in bowler hats every so often and march up and down with drum and fife making absolute arses of themselves, and all because of something Oliver Cromwell did to William the Conqueror in the year dot. I don't know about you, Bill, but I find it hard enough to remember what happened in the '39 show.

Anyway, latest flap concerns six of the RC lot who are in jug and have spent the last year or so smearing the wall with shit to get extra blankets, etc etc. Prison Governor, rather a daft-looking bloke with glasses, very reasonably told them to stop arsing about, no way to run a prison, not a zoo, etc. Now they're bent on starving themselves to death. I told Peter Carrington what I thought was the sensible thing to do, which was to shut up and let nature take its course, reductions always desirable at this time of cuts in Government expenditure, etc. Instead of which, Bill, Peter C. et al all worked themselves up into the most frightful lather: world press up in arms, foreign TV men snooping about, M's image in danger of taking a dent, etc. Some initiative in order.

Before you can say Jack Robinson, limos at the door, onto the Aer Lingus shuttle, Howe, Carrington, Atkins — he's our man in Ulster, totally out of his depth but not one to refuse a drink — Yours Truly allowed to come along for the ride, sitting in the Non-Smoking bay surrounded by what I took at first to be a bunch of unshaven thugs laden down with offensive hardware but who turned out to be our gallant lads in the SAS.

The idea, as it emerged, was a top level eyeball-to-eyeball conference in some four-star bordello near the airport with the Senior Leprechaun, a shifty little bugger by the name of Haughey, very reminiscent of that so-called gynaecologist who ran a clinic next door to Maurice Picarda's establishment during his Rubber Goods phase. O'Leary? No matter. M. inevitably taken in by the blarney within minutes. Arm round the shoulder, Jameson's in ample quantities, gales of laughter, risque anecdotes from Peter C., Howe misty-eyed recalling some obscure Irish relative of advanced years in Connemara, apparently a dab hand at the harp.

52

I tottered off at about half-one, having been bored almost to death by Atkins' tales of domestic misfortunes and deciding it was time for Bedfordshire. The following morning, imagine my surprise to find them still at it. Empty bottles as far as the eye can see, frightful fug, ashtrays overflowing, wet cigar ends, enough to make a man take the pledge. Cage opens, reptiles flood in, camera bags and reporters' notebooks at the ready. Little Haughey on his feet at once, announcing historical breakthrough, new way forward, epoch-making agreement, two great countries, etc. I could see Carrington and M. looking a bit askance, though clearly in no mood to focus. Turns out afterwards that somebody said something in the middle of the night with which they all agreed, but unfortunately in the light of day nobody for the life of them could remember what it was.

A propos your very kind enquiry. What I would really like is a new set of those Scandinavian woolly jobs from Lillywhites to keep my clubs warm. I should warn you, when you come to open my present, avoid doing so in the presence of Daphne. The Major bought it in Hamburg and I thought it might tickle your fancy.

Toodleoo for now,

DENIS

10 Downing Street
Whitehall

2 JANUARY 1981

Dear Bill,

If the following narrative appears to be slightly incoherent, I can only offer by way of mitigation the very terrible toll taken by alcohol through the system over the ten days of festivities. If I had a twenty pound note for every snort forced on me since Christmas Eve I should be a very rich man indeed. Alas, any illusion of bonhomie or optimism thus produced has now evaporated in no uncertain manner and I am left with a splitting headache and a New Year resolution to cut down by at least a couple of bottles a day.

Things started coming unpicked, as far as I can recall, on Christmas Eve when we arrived at an icy Chequers to find that Mr Woo, the very capable Filipino caretaker put in by the National Trust, had broken his leg while bringing in the coke and had been taken to hospital in Aylesbury, where he was put in the Princess Alice Memorial Ward and not expected to be up and about much before Easter. This inevitably threw the Boss into a bit of a tiswas, and for a moment or two she seriously considered taking up the Carringtons' invitation to join them and their in-laws up the road. However, this was not to be, and M. was soon on the phone to her Cockney barrow-boy friend at the *Daily Express*, who also, it now transpires, runs that ghastly hotel underneath the Chiswick Flyover where the Major stayed the night the baggage handlers went on strike at Heathrow. Little Matthews instantly obliged, and by the time we'd opened a cardboard crate or two of snorts and managed to get the Calor Gas working, a swarthy menial in a white hat had arrived and was humping various pre-cooked delicacies out of a battered van and into the deep freeze. He seemed quite perky, and I was mildly disappointed when he knocked back the proffered snort and drove off into the night, narrowly missing the local carol-singers who were advancing up the drive, escorted by a posse of police armed to the teeth with machine-guns.

Luckily M. was still in a state of some euphoria on account of the Hunger Strikers running up the white flag. Personally, I had a sneaking feeling all along that as the whiff of Christmas Pudding and warm Guinness began to circulate along the corridors of H-Block the Paddies' nerve would begin to crack. However, such has been the mood in recent months that the slightest good news brings on a fit of euphoria all round, and I was beginning to hope that it might see us through the Sacred Festival without unpleasantness. As it turned out, this was not to be.

You may have gathered from the *Telegraph* that Joe Soap at the moment is wretched old Howe, the once-ebullient sporter of the brothel-creepers and the freshly shampooed quiff. It appears that he has to carry the can for the failure of this Money Supply thing to work properly, though as neither he nor the Boss understands a blind thing about it, this strikes me as a bit unfair. There are, as you will have heard on the grapevine, a host of Whitehall Sir Hector this's and Sir Herbert thats, plus the pinstripe and brolly brigade, all chewing the rug

in the wings. Anyway, some time before the Season of Good-will, M. decided that the whole lot of them were deeply suspect, pinkoes, hobnobbers with Heath in the past, etc, and the only answer was to bring in a tame boffin hitherto hiding out as a tax exile in the US of A. As far as I can see, quite a decent bird, no different from the rest of her little band of eager beavers, except that he has a rather higher opinion of the Boss, which may explain why he is being paid the fifty thousand smackers.

However, Brother Howe had clearly got wind of the fact that he might be in for a reshuffle, and on Boxing Day — Christmas itself very quiet, both of us thank God having something cold on a tray in our respective rooms — jangle, jangle from the front door bell, enter Howe, puffing at stub of cigar, followed by talkative wife, both laden down with gifts, exuding bonhomie. Just happened to be passing on my way back to Town, taken liberty of dropping by, trust not inconvenient. No, no, not at all, what could be more delightful, kisses exchanged with talkative wife, Denis will get us something from the cellar. Meanwhile insincerity of the foregoing clearly indicated by frosty look from M., capable of freezing the balls off a snowman. H. not aware of this, however, always one to look on the bright side.

Yours truly, having lingered a while below decks to sample the Imperial Tokay laid down by old Macmillan — only decent thing he ever did — returns aloft to find M. still glacial, talkative wife examining pictures, Howe attempting to light new cigar at wrong end. Sherbets all round, comes a silence. Howe: "What a pity about John Nott." Boss: "How do you mean, what a pity about John Nott?" Howe: "I mean his getting mixed up in this Rossminster business. Sticky wicket." Another awkward silence, broken by Lady H. embarking on long range weather forecast. It may have been the tinctures, but it took me a moment or two to twig what it was that Howe was on about, and then of course the penny dropped. Friend Nott, a bald geezer with glasses and a fishy look, generally tipped as obvious Substitute waiting in the Clubroom in the event of any New Year Reshuffle. Answer, nobble Friend Nott by snide suggestions he had blotted his copybook on the Revenue front, and Brother Howe allowed to stay in Davis Cup team, he hopes.

M. refuses however to be drawn either into the fiscal misdemeanours or the meteorological stuff, and changes the subject rapidly to Fred Astaire and the BBC's Christmas package of old films, what a good impression Mike Yarwood had done of Michael Foot, etc. Bedraggled pair leave moments later still under impression their sortie has not been in vain. I put in a word for old Howe afterwards, pointing out that if anyone to be tossed to the wolves why not Heseltine or Stevarse, where real public enjoyment would be derived from the spectacle. M. however remaining tight-lipped retires to den.

Toodleoo for the nonce,

DENIS

10 Downing Street
Whitehall

16 JANUARY 1981

Dear Bill,

I expect you've all been having a jolly good chuckle about our Norman being given the heave-ho by the Boss. Personally I can't say I was over-distressed to see the back of the smarmy little bugger, although I must say it did come as a bit of a surprise, as M. has always given the impression the sun shines out of his arse, and even tolerated his so-called jokes, allowing him to refer to her as "the blessed Margaret" etc. Well, he's certainly got his come-uppance now.

Everyone seems pretty mystified here about what actually lay behind Stevarse's fall from grace. I think it had a lot to do with the arrival of M's latest recruit to the staff, an American professor called Walters. I'd just got back from the Lillywhites' Sale — where who should I run into but the widow Tremlett, rather flushed and weaving her way into the Apres Ski department on the arm of some swarthy little Greek johnny in pebble spectacles and an astrakhan overcoat — when the bell rang at Number Ten, and there was this cove on the doorstep, fresh from Heathrow with six or seven tartan suitcases on little wheels.

Needless to say, I hadn't the faintest idea who he was, and assumed him to be an emissary of that new President they've got in, Hopalong Cassidy or whatever his name is. Everyone else had gone out, so I showed him the spare room, gave him a towel and a piece of soap, and he began the lengthy task of hanging up his suits. Eventually he toddled down in a clean shirt, gleaming shoes etc, rubbing his hands and saying he wanted to get at it. I assumed he meant the drinks cabinet and ladled out a pretty lethal snorto de luxe, knowing the knack Americans have for putting it away, and poured myself a largish one to keep him company.

Emboldened by the amber fluid I broached the obvious topic — "What brings you to our shores?" It soon transpires that this is the bean there's all the talk about to be taken on at fifty grand a year to sort things out. What strikes me as odd about these chaps, like that fat old geriatric Mr Macgregor the

Monk brought in to close down British Steel at an even larger inducement, is that if they're so good at it why don't they stay in America? I was wondering whether I could formulate this in some tactful manner, and considering on balance it might be better avoided, when M. arrived, full of apologies, traffic, Whitehall absolutely chock-a-block, must be the Sales, and our American visitor began rubbing his hands again and asking when he could really get down to it in earnest.

I was just fetching some new litre bottles from the cellar when high-pitched cries and laughter from upstairs suggested that the meeting had been joined by a third party. Sure enough, it transpired that Stevarse had blown in with an enormous bouquet of flowers for the Boss from some visiting band of strolling ballet wooftahs at present throwing themselves about for the delectation of the locals at Sadlers Wells. Catching sight of the American, he became very arch. Sorry he hadn't brought him any flowers, hadn't realised he was so young, much better looking than in his photographs. I could see the Boss beginning to bridle at this line of talk, however our Papist friend seemed oblivious of the mood and plunged on. "As long as you realise, my dear" — giving him a pat on one tartan-clad knee — "you are only here as decoration, to add a bit of class to the Leaderene's entourage. Don't expect any help from us mere Cabinet Ministers, we are just a teeny bit busy what with one thing and another, and there are some of us who feel, strictly between ourselves, that all this Business Efficiency number is just a touch passe. I know you don't agree with me, Margaret" — here he leaned across and squeezed M's elbow in a disagreeably obsequious manner — "you're so delightfully twinset and pearls in your old-fashioned suburban way."

Wasn't there some bloke in Elizabethan days who was very thick with the Virgin Queen and eventually went too far, put his foot in it and got his head chopped off? I couldn't help being reminded of that scenario as I watched M's lip beginning to curl, and Stevarse rhapsodising on about how much free time our American guest was going to have and how they could go to Museums and Art Galleries together. The trouble with bachelors, Bill, is that they can never spot the storm cones being hoisted. "Thank you, Norman," the Boss eventually breathed. "That will be all. The Professor and I have some serious work to get on with. I would be grateful if you would be outside my office tomorrow morning at half-past seven with your portfolio."

Never a nice sight to see a fellow getting his cards, Bill. You remember at Burmah the occasion poor old Groggy Rossiter took one afternoon off too many and ran into Sir Hector walking through the ornamental fishpond holding his trousers? None of us had much time for him, but he did make a very pathetic sight calling in at the canteen to say his last farewells to the tea ladies. I found poor Stevarse sitting in the hall on the way down to breakfast, blubbing like a schoolboy and wiping his eyes with one of those big mauve hankies he always has floating out of his pocket, drenched inevitably in some repulsive French scent. As I said to him, it wasn't anything he'd done, merely that M. had worked herself up into a mood for human sacrifice and he just happened to be the ram caught in the thicket. He snivelled on about how he was now accused of leaking secrets, how dare she speak like that to a close friend of the Pope, and I later suggested to M. that she might drop him some sort of conciliatory line, no hard feelings etc. Not but what I'm pretty convinced she's storing up a bit of trouble for herself. If she thinks our friend Norman is now going to sit on the Back Benches preserving a dignified silence and muttering Hear Hear from time to time she is very much mistaken. Viz E. Heath, another lonely bachelor, who has no intention of burying the hatchet, except in one particular place. Say what you like about marriage, and both of us have said a good deal in our time, you do learn to forgive and forget. At least I do, even if she doesn't.

Ah me, we live in troublous times.

Yours till the cows come home,

DENIS

10 Downing Street
Whitehall

30 JANUARY 1981

Dear Bill,

Everyone cock-a-hoop at this end, as you can imagine, about the cowboy chap taking over in the Americas. As you know, I've always had my reservations about Carter ever since he started that business of walking about hand-in-hand with his wife, which suggested to me that decay in the grey cells had set in, but the new bloke looks equally rum. His hair colour is very obviously out of a bottle and M. says he's really 83, so I wouldn't give him very long in the hot seat before he turns his toes up. He has the look about him of that chap behind the bar in the Wig & Compasses on the front at Deal the Major always swore wore makeup and who keeled over shortly after marrying a wife half his age. This Reagan chap has the same decrepit painted-up air, and I fear little Mr Bush will be asked to step in e'er long. However, the Boss thinks he's absolutely the bee's knees, saying all the same things that she says and deluging her with signed photographs of himself at an earlier epoch, wearing a white hat and sitting on a horse. Not but what we have been invited over to the US of A next month to go and kiss hands in the Oval Room. I imagine it will be pretty thick with other old film stars in wigs, with a generous sprinkling of the Mafia. Hardly my idea of a Winterbreak, Bill, but M's already slavering to climb aboard the Concorde.

Meanwhile, all eyes here are focussed on the other side. I know the Boss isn't doing too well at the moment with the pollsters, but we were all pretty chuffed to discover that poor old Foot is trailing behind with only 26% knowing who he is. I put it down to his broken leg and his popping in and out of hospital all the time. No one's going to have too much confidence in a chap who seems to operate on the end of a flex from the Geriatric Ward.

(By the by, do you follow the career at all of that chap Bosanquet who used to read out the news on the other channel? He seems to rival Maurice Picarda on the drink problem front, marked tendency to blackouts and sudden insensibility due to a surfeit of snorts. Nowadays however he has trained all the Press johnnies into saying that he suffers from epilepsy, a frightfully good wheeze which I mooted to Margaret might be worth falling back on from time to time in our own private life. E.g., on visits to the Opera, "You must forgive Denis, he's been completely epileptic since teatime". M. failed to comment, and obviously didn't think it was much of a joke.)

However that may be. With repeated collapse of Uncle Michael, Red hopes are now pinned on the Big Split. I think I may have mentioned a fat chap with glasses we met in Brussels once, very up with European high society and dropping names as if there was no tomorrow. Jenkins the name, though not to be confused with that oily little Welshman with the squeaky voice who seems to make such a good living out of the Unions. Jenkins, the Brussels one, has been hovering about for some months now waiting to sound the trumpet and rally the faithful, i.e. drawing-room liberals everywhere, plus the messy-looking woman that Margaret can't stand. Latest wheeze is that they gang up with the Liberals and do some kind of deal to pull the rug from under our friend
from the geriatric ward, i.e. Old Grandpa Foot. (Quite a decent old cove, actually, as I may have said before. I see him hobbling down Whitehall from time to time, blind as a bat and always clutching a great pile of books, very like that Methodist sky pilot who was run over in Tunbridge Wells at the end of the war.) I told the Boss over tinctures the other evening not to bank on the fat cat Jenkins getting his little bandwaggon off the ground, but she thinks given a fair wind it should put the kibosh on the Opposition for the next twenty-five years or so. The ability of everyone here to look on the bright side never ceases to amaze me.

Do you notice how the Monk keeps getting pelted with eggs? No matter where he goes, there's always some little bolshie lurking with a box of Standard Whites at the ready. Never happens to any of the others. I can't understand why he goes on. Oddly enough I ran into him the other night at an extraordinary gathering organised by Saatchis at which M. entertained the Professor Branestawms of our day, all of them encouraged to bring along their inventions. I pressed him on the egg question, did he mind constantly having to wipe the yolk out of his eye, etc? Gave me a very wild look. Obviously thought I was the barmy one. After that I got talking to some cove from Barnsley who'd dreamed up a contraption for making petrol out of alcohol. I rather steered him round by the end of the evening, I think, and he promised to go home and work on it. I'll let you know if he delivers anything drinkable.

Yours aye,

DENIS

 10 Downing Street
Whitehall

13 FEBRUARY 1981

Dear Bill,

Poor old Maurice seems to have worked himself up into a shocking state about BL. I had to listen to him for an hour on the blower the other night, all through the International Golf, on the subject of his double-glazing enterprise, Picwarmth Ltd, and why it was in the hands of the Receiver. Why should Edwardes be bailed out and not him? Here we were, all being told to cut our fuel bills, Picwarmth to the rescue with some type of asbestos padding he got hold of after a big fire in Taiwan, ready to be installed by what he calls his highly-trained staff, which you or I know perfectly well is the same bunch of tearaway darkies he was using when he was in ballpoint pens, solar heating and his dispatch service, and the

Government allows him to go to the wall without so much as waving him goodbye. I didn't see the point in arguing the toss with the old boy as he was clearly in a very emotional state. Nor did I like to ask whether he was still with that fat woman from the Antique Supermarket, but there was certainly someone in the background giving him a bit of stick.

As a matter of fact I find myself pretty baffled by the Leyland caper. Our lot have always been saying that we've got to stand on our own feet, make our own way in the world, stop nannying the proles etc and now the Monk is giving a blank cheque to little Edwardes to blow on those workshy yobboes at Longbridge. If you ask me, as far as the Boss is concerned at least, it was all done by some pretty nimble PR chancers at the time of the Metro launch. Always make a pitch for the wife, these car salesmen. I remember the Major telling me it was the first rule in his book. So while I was shunted off for tinctures with a lot of silly women in leotards M. was slid in behind the wheel and encouraged to do a ton round the dirt track, photographer johnnies in attendance. When she came back she was exactly like someone who had been on the Big Dipper. Eyes gleaming, breathless, a lot of talk about shining new appliances, optional extras and eighty-three mpg, which I personally take with a pretty large pinch of salt. PR men in active negotiation with Saatchis, offering a hefty discount under the Cars for Stars scheme — you may remember that woman on the telly with the teeth got one.

You know the form, Bill. I remember you describing how Daphne set her heart on that Japanese Landrover with the eight-wheel drive and sunroof. Lot of flak, inevitably, but I managed to make the point that there are certain areas in which hubby knows best, that there was nothing wrong with the Rolls and if she wanted a runabout she always had the old Ford banger. In any case, just the kind of thing the press monkeys were bound to jump on. Peter Carrington, I must admit, was v. impressed. In his book I had steered the Boss out of what could have been a pretty sticky situation. Typically, ever since then, M. has had a soft spot for little Edwardes, and apparently the Monk has now done some sums on his pocket calculator and worked out that if they closed down the whole shebang as they intended the bill for supplementary benefits would come to more than what they're shelling out by way of largesse as it is. So there.

Meanwhile you might have thought that it would have

stopped the Boss in her tracks. Not a bit of it. She is now firing on fifteen cylinders, enemies swatted like flies on all sides. It's a horrifying sight to see her eyes gleaming as she leaves Number Ten, ready for the afternoon scrap with poor old Foot — on the ropes already and clearly beginning to wish he'd stuck to antiquarian book-selling. (I was told the other day that it was his wife who put him up to it in the first place, which doesn't surprise me.) Ditto the smelly socks brigade. Little Len Murray dragged in again with his five point plan for putting things to rights, brutally savaged by the Boss and quickly dragged out of the cage by his friends waving chairs to create a diversion.

I suppose you've noticed. Front page of the *Telegraph*. This Roy Rogers character holding hands with his wife already. Just like Carter. At the age of seventy, I find that pretty obscene. I can't believe he'll last. However, more of that when we hit Washington.

I got your message about me picking up one of those American walkie-talkie telephones for the garden when I'm over there. Is there anything else you wanted on the leisure front? Saatchis are apparently providing us with some spending money.

Yours in the Lord,

DENIS

10 Downing

27 FEBRUARY 1981

Dear Bill,

I don't know whether you spotted this snap of yours truly in the *Telegraph* last week, but I enclose it for your delectation.

What happened was somewhat unfortunate. Do you remember that rather sharp little cove, Courtauld, who manages the gents' sportswear department at Lillywhites? I was in there the other day picking up some new togs, when up he bustles rubbing his hands no end and saying I might be interested in their new line in Apres Golf wear. Assistant summoned forward wearing tartan-lined Sherlock Holmes number, much favoured by the aristocracy, etc, prepared to make a very generous reduction. A glance in the full-length mirror was enough to convince me I'd clearly get the bird at Littlestone, but as it was a cold day and, if I am to be entirely frank, I may have imbibed a little too freely over luncheon at the RAC, a credit card changed hands and before I knew it my old dirty mac had been packed up in a suitcase and I was bowling off along Jermyn Street attracting wolf whistles from every side.

Needless to say, there were the usual Press Scum lurking in the bushes outside Number Ten, blaze of flashlights and I entered dazzled to encounter a straight left from M. What on earth did I think I was playing at? Look what happened to Wilson when he started modelling macs for the Estonian jailbird, take it off this minute, bloody fool, etc. So that was that. Courtauld was v. apologetic down at Lillywhites, offered me a credit note, but it didn't seem the same somehow so I blew it all on a row of stiff ones round the corner in the Ritz Bar.

I've been trying to keep out of the way as much as possible in view of what's been happening with the Miners. The Boss is in a prickly state at present and best left alone anyway. I began to smell a rat when little Pym got up on his hind legs. (Quite a decent bird who I think may have been at Eton with Sticky's elder brother, the one who was cashiered for that nasty business in Benghazi.) I've always found him very sound on keeping the lower orders in their place, hence my alarm when he gets up and begins spouting about adjustments and the need to bend with the wind. Apparently old Humpty-Dumpty Thorneycroft sounded off along the same lines. Next thing that happens, a perfectly sensible decision is taken to shut down twelve or so coal-mines in the Rhondda Valley where they've been losing money since the First World War. Whereupon the Taffys rise in rage, shut up shop before it's shut up for them, and light the braziers outside the gates.

I could see the Boss was beginning to show signs of panic but in view of the fact that the black-faced boyos had yet to receive the blessing of Uncle Joe Gormley I advised her to sit tight and await developments, ideally large brownie in hand.

The point I made, Bill, is that they could easily see off a full-scale revolt, huge mountains of coal having been piled up all over Wales for the simple reason they can't sell the stuff. The Major was telling me only the other day that he'd been down to that coal merchant friend of his in Swindon, and even with the ten per cent off for old times' sake a ton of smokeless briquettes still set the poor old boy back a hundred quid, and most of that was rock. No wonder, then, the miners have lit up the braziers, having to shift it somehow. (You must be thanking your lucky stars you went over to the log-burner. Precious little chance of the lumberjacks coming out.)

Meanwhile, back at the seat of power, all would have been well, I surmise, if Peter Carrington had managed to keep his nerve. As I may have said before, he's a very decent little cove, but I had forgotten the fact that he went through all that ghastly business when he and Heath shut the country down four days a week, and he still wakes up in the middle of the night screaming at the thought of Joe Gormley. At the first sign of trouble he appears at the Talking Shop, pale at the gills. I must say, I award him high marks for guile, though. Straight in to the Boss, advising her to emulate her predecessor Heath. Stand up to the buggers. Heath very wise in many ways, history will vindicate him, could probably be persuaded to come round to Downing Street and lend a hand. As you well know, Bill, any mention of the seafaring bachelor is like a red rag to a bull, and Margaret's response was predictable enough. Little Howell, the Energy chap, was instantly whistled in and told to run up the white flag. Carrington grinning up his sleeve like a Cheshire Cat, and finally accepting my offer of a very large one.

Do you remember that poetry book we had at Mill Hill, Bill? There were some very good lines in it by someone or other to the effect that once you start paying out money to the Danes you'll never get rid of the buggers. I told Carrington this. What about the Sewage Wallahs? I said. They'll be on the rampage next. What are we supposed to do then: stop going to the lavatory? Carrington was very condescending, as much as saying in so many words I didn't understand what I was talking about, compromise was the name of the game and we had to show we'd got a human face, just like that woman with the bad haircut they've all got their knickers in a twist about.

We're just off to the Land of the Free to see Old Hopalong. I still can't get used to the idea of him being in the White House. Imagine if Kenny Moore had got the Boss's job, you'd think it pretty rum, wouldn't you, Bill?

So long, my friend, and may the Good Lord take a liking to you.

Yours,

DENIS

Dear Bill,

I hope you got the duty-free Bourbon. I asked one of Carrington's lackeys to drop it off at the Club. Unfortunately the Walkie-Talkie Telephone you wanted for Daphne was re-routed to Seattle owing to a baggage mix-up, but it may turn up in the fullness of time. I would have done more about it, but I am still somewhat under the weather thanks to jet-lag et al.

I can't remember whether you've ever crossed the Big Pond, Bill, but the first thing that strikes you from a cultural point of view is their extraordinary drinking habits. The first night we got there -- as you know, it's earlier when you arrive than when you take off, and I couldn't entirely make out whether it was yesterday or tomorrow back home, but not to worry — we drove up to the White House all spruced up in bib and tucker on the stroke of seven. Greeted by the most godawful fanfare from *Call Me Madam* played by a lot of Marines in ill-fitting uniforms with their hats slipping over their ears. The Major had warned me not to expect too much on the drill and turn-out front when it came to ceremonial. Old Hopalong standing at the top of the steps, as I feared holding hands with the First Lady — but I was damned if I was going to follow suit. We were then ushered into a darkened room full of very old film stars, some of whom I vaguely recognised from the black and white talkie days.

I had just been introduced to that rather nice old bean who plays golf and used to do a double act with Bing Crosby before he turned his toes up, when a big black man in some sort of mediaeval costume eased forward with a trayful of long-stemmed goblets and asked me whether I would prefer a Shot Bulldog or a Copacabana Fizz. I could see with my practised eye that there were obviously no bona fide snorts to hand so I took pot luck with what I surmised to be a bit of everything poured into a glass and covered with grated coconut. Absolutely lethal, at least after half a dozen or so. The trouble is, you see, that having got you there at tea-time,

Brother Yank doesn't believe in getting his nose into the trough much before 10pm, by which time one and all are absolutely pie-eyed.

No wonder when it came to the speeches they were a touch over the top. Hopalong kicked off with the most balls-aching encomium of the Bulldog Breed, apparently under the impression that Winston Churchill was still alive, and comparing the Boss to Boadicea standing up to the Trots. (The news of the miners' cave-in didn't seem to have penetrated to their neck of the woods, which was probably just as well under the circs.) M. then sprang to her feet, eyes blazing in the candle-light, telling Hopalong that he was the best thing since sliced bread and that should he feel like nuking the Ayatollah or any of the other Middle Eastern monkeys we would be delighted to place the entire Royal Air Force at his disposal. I could see poor little Carrington going white about the gills and burying his head in his hands, but this could have been the effect of the Bulldogs.

By the time the Boss had finished it was six in the morning by my watch, and I was looking forward to a spot of Bedford-shire. However it was not to be. Tables cleared by more gigantic Uncle Toms in fancy dress, cigarettes lit, and the Mafia man with the toupee was wheeled on to sing his Hundred Best Tunes. At this point the Hollywood geriatrics began to show signs of life, and Hopalong led Margaret onto the dancefloor for a smooch. I was aware that eyes were turning in my direction and it eventually dawned on me that I was expected to do my bit with the First Lady. I can't say I enjoyed it, but we did a couple of circuits without either of us falling over. I tried to explain how the Queen wasn't really in charge, as they all seem to think, but the old girl clearly wasn't concentrating and conversation rather dried up after that.

The next day there was a return match at the British Embassy, with the same cast, and I was sorry to see that our chaps, presumably out of deference to the natives, were proffering the same kind of poisonous rubbish in the way of booze — tomato sauce mixed with brandy and grated choco-late, I think it was. Same speeches, M. comparing Hopalong to Abraham Lincoln, Hopalong proposing toast to King George VI, Mafia man wheeled out to sing identical selection, and the same nausea on the dancefloor to wind things up, except that Reagan on this occasion was being followed round in the Slow

Waltz by his medico carrying a little black bag. I must say, Bill, he does look very rum. His hair is a funny kind of orange colour, make-up half an inch thick coming off on his collar, very like one of those figures in the Waxworks. When he speaks it's really uncanny. I formed the impression he has very little idea of what's going on. The only time he spoke to me he seemed to think I was Peter Carrington.

I had been hoping for a round of golf and a snort or twain with the old Bing man, but I was shunted off with a bunch of expatriate businessmen, all total abstainers, who were under the impression that the one thing I wanted to see was some old battlefield to do with *Gone With The Wind*. The only explanation I could think of was that they'd got me mixed up in the card index with poor old Enoch, who does indeed take an interest in such antiquarian matters. I was jolly glad to get back on the Concorde, have a decent unadulterated snort and head for home. The Boss seemed very geared up by the whole thing, only Carrington sitting in the back seat by the lavatory looking out of the window in a pretty sombre mood. He turned out to be right, as we got back to find the Arabs all trotting out the usual, saying they could get on quite nicely without our armed assistance and turning over all their order books for future weaponry to Giscard. Ah me.

We meet I think on the night of the 12th for the Inner Wheel do at Tunbridge Wells. I have alerted Fatty Farmer who is providing beds.

Have a nice day,

DENIS

10 Downing Street
Whitehall

27 MARCH 1981

Dear Bill,

Lot of rumpus as you may have seen this week about another weirdo in the FO being caught with his trousers down. I don't know what it is about the Foreign Office, but it does seem to attract the dirty raincoat brigade in very large numbers. Makes you wonder when they get down to any work. Do you remember that retired Nautical Attache who lived down the road from the Major? Used to come into the Saloon Bar as regular as clockwork on the stroke of six in a floor-length evening gown and a hat with flowers on, expecting to be called Vera. Now, I gather, he's a disc-jockey in Bangkok. I am beginning to look at Carrington in a new light.

You may have thought the Boss had got her back to the wall with all this shindig over the Budget. Not a bit of it. Apparently the Wets kicked up a stink about not being told in advance about the 20p on petrol but I don't see why they didn't look in the papers and read it there like everyone else. Not but what it wasn't a fairly stormy session. I always think I'm fairly well sound-proofed wrapped around a bottle of Gordon's up here in the attic, but the Proprietorial tones penetrated as clear as a bell. I think old Farmer Prior got the worst of it, closely followed by Gilmour. I don't know if you've seen him on TV at all, a streaky version of little Carrington with a face like a cemetery on a wet afternoon and a wife who is the spitting image of Margaret, which can't be much consolation to him when he toddles home at night after a thumping from the Boss.

M's repeated argument, on a point of housekeeping, is that they can't go on borrowing money, what would the neighbours think, etc? I can't quite understand the logic of this, Bill. I don't know whether you've seen the adverts in the *Telegraph* for National Savings, but they are now offering something like 14% tax-free, and I've been seriously thinking of shifting my little nest-egg from Brother Furniss at the NatWest. Though having seen a bit of the way these characters go on I am hesitant to trust them with my own money, and Furniss does keep a very decent bottle of Amontillado in the safe, which you won't get from the Giro. My argument, however, is that if that isn't borrowing, what is?

73

One point is they all now admit that this money supply thing they've been on about ever since they got in is a total non-starter. The idea was that if you brought down the money supply, whatever that means, inflation would come down as well. Now, even despite their efforts, inflation has come down a bit but the money supply has gone up. I asked little Howe, busy though he obviously was, whether he could perhaps enlighten me. He was very huffy and told me to go and ask that American chap with the tartan suitcases, Walters. Pressed, however, and trapped in a corner of M's sitting-room, he burbled on a bit about how everything was going to bottom out soon, and it was all going according to plan, but that it was sometimes difficult to understand what the hell the civil servants thought they were doing.

If you ask me, the 20p petrol wheeze was all a plot dreamed up by the Boss in cahoots with her little friend Edwardes. You remember they gave her the old soap when she went up to Birmingham for the Metro launch at the Motor Show, 93 miles a gallon and all that caper. I have absolutely nothing concrete to go on, but I strongly suspect that we are now all supposed to throw up our hands in horror at 150p a gallon, cash in our old bangers, leave the Rolls to rust in the garage, etc, and invest in one of their ghastly little sardine boxes. M. keeps going on to me about how we should fly the flag and how I would find it ideal, clubs in the back, etc, mentioning various shades from Lilac to Autumn Gold, but I am resisting it and, anyway, what's 20p these days? The doorman at the Ritz literally spat at Maurice Picarda last week for giving him a five-pound note.

Anyway, the only upshot of the whole shemozzle was this poor idiot Brocklebank-Something who's so wet you could flush him down the khasi and never notice, trickling across the floor to join Fatty Jenkins' merry little band of gastronomes. If that's the calibre of recruit they're going for I think Margaret would be justified in spending a bit of money on doing up Chequers for a fairly long stay.

This would amuse you, Bill. One of the Coons popped in last week, offering to buy several million pounds' worth of British hardware as long as we'd lend them the money to pay for it. I sat next to the Sultana at dinner and put in a word for Maurice P's double-glazing. She said they didn't have anything like that in Nigeria, so it could be his big chance.

Yours in hope,

DENIS

Dear Bill,

What about Hopalong getting hit in the shoulder, just like all his old films? I gather it was done by some nutcase who thought he was in a Western. I suppose in a country like America, given their drinking habits, most of the time they have no idea whether it's real or on television anyway. No wonder they all go round the bend and start shooting each other at the drop of a hat. Margaret sent a telegram of condolence but hasn't had a reply yet. There's a feeling at this end that the old boy may in fact be in worse shape than they're letting on. After all, he is seventy and you remember how long Archie Wellbeloved took to get over it when he shot himself through the foot whilst trying to rid the church of sparrows during Evensong.

Talking of Archie, I gave him a ring the other night to ask his advice about who they should have as the new Bishop of London. Margaret had got her knickers in a tremendous twist about Runcie trying to bring in yet another of his various stooges and I told her to leave it to me. Archie, who may be pretty senile but still has his ear to the ground, came up with this fellow from Truro who, he assures me, is very sound on women priests and cracking down on our gay friends, of whom, if you ask me, there is a pretty fair sprinkling in ecclesiastical circles. I passed this on to the Boss, and you will be glad to hear it has gone through, despite considerable tantrums and slamming down of the receiver at Buck House on account of Truro once having administered a public wigging to Princess Margaret when she was carrying on with that nancy-boy pop singer.

Meanwhile they're all over the moon here about the new ructions on the other side. Just when poor old Foot thought he was in for a week or two of peace and quiet now that Jenkins and his little crew have set sail in the good ship Social Democrat, up pops Benn in the middle of the night, eyes rotating like Catherine Wheels, and announces he is going to oust Healey from the Number Two spot. My own view, con-

sidering the lateness of the hour and the emotional stability of the subject, was that Benn had had a few in the Members' Bar and was sounding off as many of us do in the small hours following the ingestion of more than the usual skinful. In our case, Bill, we forget about it altogether next morning, and no harm done. It turned out, however, that Benn had total recall and meant every word of it. I must say, my heart goes out to poor old Foot. He must be beginning to regret ever embarking on such a wretched old age. As I may have said before, I think it was his wife who put him up to it. There he could have been still, wandering about on Hampstead Heath, taking the dog for a walk, browsing through his second-hand bookshops, not a care in the world: instead he must be up at the crack of dawn, hardly time for a shit and a shave, and straight into battle with Benn or the Boss. What a life!

However, what's sauce to the goose does something or other to the gander, and M. is happy as a grig about the Benn affair, predicting fifty years of glorious rule, golden jubilee celebrations etc and the Winston treatment when it finally comes to the wooden box.

I must say I thought she would have caught her breath when a round robin was delivered last week by 364 economists all telling her that she was barking up the wrong tree. It did look quite an impressive list, for length if nothing else, and I noted that Margaret did at least peruse it briefly just to see if Walters — the American chap with the tartan suitcases — had also appended his monicker. Having assured herself that he had not, she then passed it on to some skivvy from the Press Office to make hay of it in the usual manner. The official line was that it was all got up by those two old Hungarian comics who used to advise Wilson, what did they know about it, if they were so smart why weren't they rich, etc?

A propos all that, I bumped into a chap in the Club the other day called Smithers who was at school with Picarda's rich brother-in-law, and seemed to be something of a big noise in Threadneedle Street. He said they're all raring to go. Recession lifting, light at the end of the tunnel, everything will be all right on the night, have another one and why not make it a double? I told him, while accepting his generous offer for the sake of politeness, that that wasn't my view from where I was sitting, but in my experience it's something to do with the buds coming out. I went in to see Furniss at the NatWest the other day, and he was in very much the same state of euphoria, hitting the Amontillado as if there was no tomorrow. Ah well, it takes all snorts, as the Major's mother used to say, God rest her soul.

I have rented a little place on Sandwich Bay for Easter. Any chance of making up a foursome for a stroll round Royal St George's? M. promises me she will definitely be in Brussels, hammering out the fish.

Take care.

Yours until the cows come home, and by the way, how is Daphne?

DENIS

KHAZI HILTON
RIYADDH S. ARABIA

24 APRIL 1981

Dear Bill,

Crikey! What a Godforsaken dump this is. Sand as far as the eye can see, wogs swarming about as if they owned the place, all the women wearing black dust-sheets, and not a snort in sight. If you want one, you have to ring the British Embassy and it's sent round in a locked van with motorcycle escort. Luckily Carrington warned me about the form, and I rigged up a kind of false golf-bag with a few sawn-off ping-irons visible at the top and all the rest suitably cushioned bottle space. I got a pretty odd look from the Chief Wog's frisker at the airport, an ex-Wingco in the RAF, who said: "If it's golf you're after you've come to the wrong shop, old fruit." I said we were stopping off in Grand Canary on the way home. Apparently if they catch you at it you're strapped over a barrel in the marketplace and given fifty lashes so I am being extremely circumspect.

India, or it may have been Pakistan, was an absolute washout. You may wonder why we keep traipsing off to these far-flung corners of the globe. I certainly do. It's all the fault of the Foreign Office as far as I can see. Margaret clearly hasn't a blind idea what she's doing, but there's always a bevy of Whitehall johnnies with briefcases waiting at the airport, bumsucking away at the locals in the most shameless manner, trying to flog them all kinds of ball-bearings, tractors, guns and that kind of thing, with Margaret just being the cherry on the cake.

I knew she wouldn't take to that Gandhi woman. She never really warmed to Golda Meir either. She can't forgive either of them for getting there first. As we got out of the aeroplane at Benares or Calcutta or wherever it was, it was like stepping into the Hot Room at the old Turkish Bath in Jermyn Street, and within seconds my drip-dry was soaking wet. The Boss had made a big effort, some little number run up by Tropicana of Piccadilly, but was clearly beginning to wilt within seconds, whereas Mother India was breezing about in a long floaty number with nothing much underneath, looking as cool as a cucumber in a pair of Chanel sunglasses. Advantage Mrs G.

By the by, Bill, it's very confusing about her being called Mrs Gandhi. I asked her about her father, assuming, as you would have done, that he was the little spindly fellow in the loincloth who was always lying down on a bed of nails in the path of oncoming trains. Not a bit of it. She told me in a rather huffy way that her old man was Pundit Nero, the one who used to wear a pillbox hat with a rose in his buttonhole and was so thick with Mountbatten's good lady. Jolly confusing, what?

The banquet was very much what you would expect, a touch of the old Raj, curry and turbans, only enlivened by a frightful shouting match between M. and the Gandhi woman, both at it like a pair of fishwives. All the Indians are up in arms about Whitelaw's latest scheme to stem the immigrant tide. On that leg of the trip the drink laws still hadn't begun to bite, and owing to jetlag I may have been over-enthusiastic about putting my oar in. I told our dusky hostess that in view of recent events in Brixton we just couldn't afford to let in a whole lot more of her compatriots. All industrious, charming little fellows, etc, but put them in South London and in no time at all they'd be bunging bricks at the Constabulary like some country coconut shy. Not that I can say I blame them.

Whereupon, Bill, solids hit the punkah. Gandhi woman rises to her feet, eyes blazing, pointing out that all her mob are quiet as mice, running newspaper shops and colonising Bradford. Brixton lot an inferior breed altogether, mad as coots, high on drugs, etc, wouldn't let them into her sub-continent in a million years, etc.

Back at the Maharajah Hilton, the Boss v. critical of my intervention, telephone calls made to British Consul, yours truly packed off on two-day sightseeing tour of the Himalayas. Actually not a bad time at all. My escort was an old chum of the Major's, chotah pegs for White Sahib very much in evidence, and my memories somewhat confused.

Here we are, however, in Wogland. My God, Bill, it's no exaggeration to say that it's literally the arsehole of the universe. No wonder poor old Picarda came unstuck when he flew out here on his chemical toilet caper. The Chief Wog, King Khaled by name, is a funny little bird in dark glasses and one of those dishcloths. M. and I poled up to the Palace only to discover the old boy had popped out to see one of his relatives having his arm chopped off for fornication, and when he got back he refused to talk to M. on the grounds that she was a woman.

We had strict instructions from Peter Carrington on no account to offend them this time, as they could cut off the supply of Four-Star at the drop of a hat. I was therefore sent in to haggle with His Nibs. The FO bloke in tow, not the brightest of sparks, did most of the talking and spent a good half hour trying to interest the King in the idea of a Gulf Force. From what I could gather, this was to consist of one old RAF Hercules on standby at Gatwick in case of Russian attack anywhere in the Middle East. Old Sheepseyes sat there pretty impassively, said nothing at all, and in the end we buggered off. M. very displeased, who did we think we were, etc? I pointed out that at least we hadn't given offence as far as I could tell, and that with any luck the oil would continue to flow.

I looked into the possibility of double-glazing for Maurice's sake, but as none of the houses have any windows I think it may be a bit of a non-starter.

See you back in Civilisation.

Yours aye,

DENIS